youth rugby
101 *drills*

chris sheryn

youth rugby

drills

A & C Black • London

First published in 2006 by
A & C Black Publishers Ltd
38 Soho Square, London W1D 3HB
www.acblack.com

ISBN-10: 0 7136 7802 X
ISBN-13: 978 0 7136 7802 4

A CIP catalogue record for this book is available from the British Library.

Note: It is always the responsibility of the individual to assess his or her own fitness capability before participating in any training activity. While every effort has been made to ensure the content of this book is as technically accurate as possible, neither the author nor the publishers can accept responsibility for any injury or loss sustained as a result of the use of this material.

Cover illustration © Alex Williamson

A & C Black uses paper produced with elemental chlorine-free pulp, harvested from managed sustainable forests.

Typeset in 10/12pt DIN regular by Palimpsest Book Production Ltd, Grangemouth, Stirlingshire
Printed and bound in Great Britain by MPG Books Ltd, Bodmin

CONTENTS

ACKNOWLEDGEMENTS

This book is an amalgamation of ideas and experiences from a number of different coaches from both league and union codes. For their help with this project I would like to thank the following: David Jackson, for some inspirational ideas on introducing tackling and defence; Simon Scull, who has proven to be a great help on all areas, especially goal-kicking; particular thanks to Wyn Sheryn, who has been the fellow burner of midnight oil. Wyn has been coaching a range of ages and sports over the past 40 years – from schoolboys to Olympians. He is currently working in not-so-semi-retirement at Hutton Grammar School in Preston introducing 11-year-olds to the great game. It is from his work there with Alf Odie that many of these drills spring.

INTRODUCTION

This book is designed to provide group leaders with a resource to construct effective frameworks within which young players (under the age of 16) can develop the skills required for rugby union. The focus is on the *basic* skills and concepts that should be at the heart of any good player's game, and for this reason you will see an emphasis on the themes of movement and core passing and catching skills. Highly complex, advanced tactical drills have not been included as they are not appropriate for this age group.

Experiences in the important early years of life can determine whether or not children continue to play into adult life and can, in many cases, colour their view of sport in general. It is therefore important to remember that the key objective for any training session with children is to create an environment to which the players want to return. I hope that the drills and ideas in this book will help to produce sessions that are stimulating, productive and above all fun for all concerned, including you, their coach.

SESSION GUIDELINES

Understanding the younger player

It is now generally accepted that pre-adolescent players require special handling and should not simply be treated as 'mini-adults'. For physiological as well as psychological reasons, training sessions must take account of the fact that children have different requirements.

It is important to remember that children will reach puberty at different ages – the chronological age for one adolescent may be up to five years out of sequence with a counterpart of the same age. It is therefore imperative that those organising group training sessions should not assume that all players are equal in physical ability or capacity.

Pre-adolescents

Generally speaking, pre-adolescent children are flexible and weak in relative terms. It is therefore not necessary to get them to do any formal flexibility work. They also are, by nature, aerobic animals. They have no anaerobic capacity so it is not appropriate for them to do any separate formal strengthening work.

However, their rugby 'technical' work should emphasise appropriate movement patterns which in themselves will have a strengthening effect, e.g. throwing activities to strengthen and teach appropriate patterns of movement. As it is an age where habits are learned, it is a good idea to encourage movements that will be used in later life.

Adolescents

Adolescents are generally the opposite to their younger counterparts in respect to their overall physical profile – they are relatively strong and inflexible. These characteristics will be more pronounced during growth spurts. Flexibility work is a good idea, and specific attention should be made to the hamstrings and calf muscles (especially during and just after growth spurts, when muscle length can lag behind increases in long bone length). Tightness in these muscle groups has been linked to episodes of anterior knee pain – especially common in adolescent girls.

> **For Example**
> Demonstrating a skill with your back to another pitch with players running around will mean that your group will have varying degrees of focus on you. Be aware of what is going on behind you. If you are introducing young children to catching practice it is a good idea to ensure that the backdrop to the object ball is uncluttered, or at least as still as possible.

Appealing to the senses

Children can process information from several senses all at once, many of which can be used to enhance learning. Different children will place a different emphasis on each sense and you need to be aware of this when coaching a skill. For example – when teaching a player to kick a ball, consider:

- **Visual** – body shapes
- **Tactile** – how the ball feels on the foot at point of impact
- **Aural** – what sound is made when the skill is well executed

By asking the children to describe their own perception of the skill during practice, a coach can build an understanding of which learning strategies the players are using, and use this knowledge to better communicate.

For Example

To ensure that the correct elements are retained for use in the drills following demonstration, the effective coach will emphasise the ONE coaching point, repeat it, demonstrate it, and then reinforce it so that when the group breaks up there is no doubt as to the element for practice.

How best to learn

Traditionally the teaching of a skill has been approached by simple repetition, in the understanding that practice makes perfect. However, research has shown that while some simple repetition for the complete beginner is beneficial, varied practice can provide faster and more permanent results.

For example, when teaching to throw into the line-out, faster progression can be made by varying the points to which the hooker is throwing – long, short, lobbed, flat etc. rather than standing and aiming at a single point repeatedly.

It is thought that the extra return could be due to the requirement to constantly revisit and most importantly adapt, driving the skill to a deeper level of under-standing. The fact that the player is being presented with different problems to solve means that the ability to adapt learned skills develops.

The learning curve

The development of a skill during a group practice will not follow a straight line. It is normal for awareness and concentration to be high initially, and for skills to develop accordingly. However, as the drill progresses, concentration levels will fall as will the accuracy of execution. If allowed to continue unchecked by the coach, competency levels will suffer.

To address this issue, coaches must constantly be aware of the pattern and take time to rest the players' minds and bodies. Stop the drill, re-communicate the objective and the skill and then once the players are rested and ready – both mentally and physically – start again. In this way the inevitable decline in competency can be halted, and the development curve can edge upwards once again.

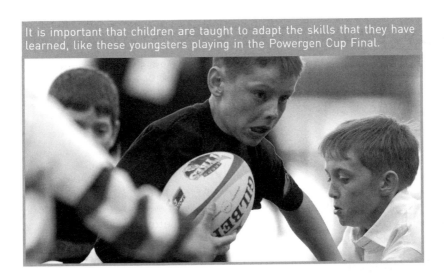
It is important that children are taught to adapt the skills that they have learned, like these youngsters playing in the Powergen Cup Final.

Coaching styles

There are about as many coaching styles as there are coaches. It is not the intention here to dictate or pass any judgment on the relative benefits of one style over another. However, it is worth considering the alternatives, and the approach that is most appropriate for you. For the coach to be aware of the variety of coaching styles can only make things more interesting for all concerned.

What follows is a summary of two main approaches, but in reality the most appropriate will be your personal blend of the two. Whatever your style, bear in mind that young players all have one thing in common – they prefer to play than practice, so make sure that sessions are fun. A sense of humour on the pitch is essential as it not only keeps the coach sane, but also removes tension that can make players less inclined to extend themselves and risk making mistakes.

- **Coach in control** – this sees the coach organising and teaching in a highly structured environment. The players will be told the focus of the drill and the relevance to the game.
- **Children in control** – this model challenges the children to decide what to learn based on what is seen as important. From a controlled game environment, a development point is identified between the coach and the children. This becomes the emphasis for the session.

Traditionally the coach has been in control of the objectives of practice and has not required the children to become too involved. Clearly there must be a balance and the effective coach will blend the two and subtly guide the children.

The limitations of this approach is one of overall control and available time, but it does offer the following advantages:

- Goals are set in line with confidence
- Players are engaged in more thought, and therefore learn more readily
- Children can be encouraged to develop self-coaching techniques which will be of great value to their own learning strategies.

This self-coaching principle can be introduced by skill practices being observed by one player/group that have a clear checklist of skills. This list will be the same cues that were emphasised during demonstration and coach-led introductions. This technique means that awareness of key learning points continues even when not directly participating. It also teaches observation skills which can be transferred to self-observation and to other groups.

Communication

In any sport, and on most training days, you will see a coach working with young players struggling to form groups into pre-drill formations. Instructions such as 'get into a circle' or 'I need two staggered lines' result in formations that owe more to a stage farce than a rugby session. This leads to exasperated coaches, confused children and wasted time. Never fear – here are some tips to help overcome some common problems:

Watch your language

I know an excellent tennis coach who, when working with a group of 6–8-year-olds, told them to 'stand in the tramlines'. I mentioned to him afterwards that the reason that not all of them responded was because they had no idea what a tram was, and even less of an idea about the area of court to which he was referring.

Try at all times to take account of the age and experience of players before you speak, avoid jargon like the plague, explain what you mean and constantly question and re-evaluate your use of language. If you want to test yourself, ask a non-rugby player to watch a session, and keep a list of all the terms that they do not understand. Have a look at the list and ask yourself what you really meant. For example, *drift, peel, drive, blind-side, punt* and *grubber* are just a few of the terms that you may use, but may not be easily understood by the younger players.

- **Get into pairs/groups of three**. This instruction will rarely illicit a prompt response as junior politics will come into play ('where's my best friend?'), and few want to take the initiative to move around and find a partner. For young children the best way to do this is to designate two points (or markers) as 'one' and 'two', then simply touch each player on the head, look them in the eye (important!) and give them a number. As soon as a player has a number they should go and stand at the marker. As the children get older you can pair them up by asking everyone to put their hand in the air and keep it there until they have a partner. In this way it is easier for everyone to see who remains.
- **Make a circle**. Ask a group of players (of any age) to form a circle, and what you will end up with will most likely resemble a football crowd. A good way to achieve an evenly spaced circle is to simply get all the players to hold hands and then slowly walk backwards as far as they can without letting go. If holding hands elicits too much schoolboy humour then they can grab jersey cuffs instead.
- **Form a staggered line**. In a number of the drills in this book you will need to form two parallel lines of players who are alternately spaced – a zigzag formation. This, again, can be a real struggle. The easy way to do this is in four steps:

1 Ask the players to form a single line and then hold hands/cuffs

2 Spread them out until they can only just hold on to each other – they will then be evenly spaced.
3 Give each consecutive player a number one or two
4 All number ones stand still. All number twos walk out to form the second line. When both lines turn to face each other you have the perfect 'zigzag'.

Group size

Consider the size of the group, and how much time each player will be waiting in line. You will need to balance appropriate rest periods with the risk of players getting cold or distracted. This will involve a bit of trial and error, but smaller is generally better as you will want to stop the drills every now and then anyway to reassert objectives and coaching points.

Quality before quantity

Building an environment of excellence can be achieved without becoming boring. Just be very clear and concise about what the skills are that you are about to practice, and then concentrate on the quality of execution at all times. Do not be drawn into lengthy drills that test stamina and reduce the quality of play – short, sharp, top quality drills engrain top quality play. Remember: 'Practice does not make perfect; it makes permanent.'

Session structure

There are as many ways to compile a session as there are coaches. There are however some guidelines that will help a session make sense for players and coaches alike. A one hour session might look like this:

1 Warm up (10 mins)

Get body and mind ready for the session to come.

2 Conditioned games (15 mins)

Plenty of fun and energy, so don't stop the action too much – only when some order is required.

3 Drills (25 mins)

Try and focus in on one common skill even if using more than one drill so that everyone is clear at the end of the session what has been learned.

4 Warm down and flexibility (10 mins)

Don't skimp on this. Young players will have less need for flexibility development but as a habit, warming down is invaluable. This is also a great opportunity to reaffirm what has just been practised and key learning points (i.e. 'we've just seen the value of driving onto the ball in the conditioned game and how communication makes the job that much easier').

NB: If you have a group of players that are involved in competitive games, you might choose to swap stages 2 and 3 around if the area for practice has already been identified. The conditioned games would then reflect the drills.

Equipment

The drills will require the following equipment:

- Cones
- Rugby balls (as many as you can lay your hands on)
- 2 x soccer balls (referred to in the drills as footballs)
- Bibs
- Tackle bags
- 6–8 old tyres

Improvising equipment

There are few groups that enjoy unlimited budgets, so here are some ideas for ways to improvise kit.

Ideal	Alternatives
Cones	Margarine lids and some poster paint to provide colour designations when required.
Tackle bags	Old MOD kit bags stuffed with rags are fine for smaller players. Stuffing them with scrap upholstery leather gives weight and realism to the bag. It takes a bit of searching out but is fantastic if you can get it. Make sure that buckles are removed for safety.
Bibs	Old T-shirts with the necks and arms cut off, treated with cold water dyes and spray painted letters. This might not look too grand, but is great fun for kids to make and saves lots of money.

WARMING UP

Working on sprinting and balance skills in warm-up drills leads to tries on the pitch – Italy's Kaine Robertson leaves France's Christophe Dominici in his wake to score in a Six Nations match.

drill 1 ball thief

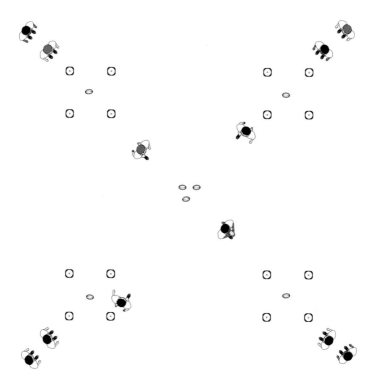

Objective: To develop communication skills and speed.

Equipment: 16 cones and eight balls.

Description: At each corner of a square (about 5 m wide) make a 1 m square with four cones – these will be the 'home base' for each team. Divide the players into four teams and stand them in line, one team behind each base. Place eight balls in the centre of the square. On the coach's command, one player from each team runs to the centre to grab one (and only one) ball before returning to base to place it in their square. Then the next player in line sets off to grab another ball. Once all the balls have gone from the centre the runners can steal a ball from the other bases. This continues until one team has three balls in their home base. If no-one wins within a set time the coach can add another ball to make success a little easier.

Coaching points: Watch for cheats picking up two balls at a time. Encourage each team to talk to their runner to make him aware of what else is going on.

drill 2 *shuttles*

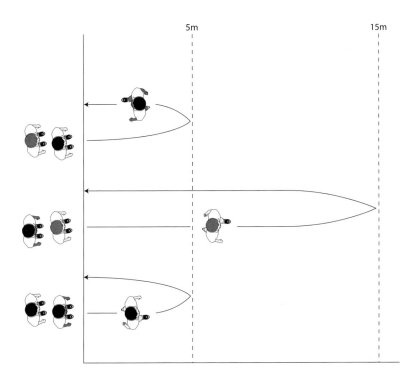

Objective: To warm up the body and practise pushing off on one foot to change direction and keep movement balanced.

Equipment: Players.

Description: Players line up along the touchline. On the coach's whistle, the players jog to the 5 m line, then turn to return to the touchline by pushing off on their landing foot and turning their shoulders to transfer the balance of weight and change direction. Players then jog to the 15 m line, performing the same action to turn.

Coaching points: Watch for a tendency to forget to change direction by pushing off on one foot and turning the shoulders, which reduces the player's balance.

Progression: Jog to the first line then sprint back, always maintaining a balanced change of direction. Pair up the players and run shuttles in relay. Player 1 jogs or sprints to the 5 m line, sprints back and player 2 repeats, and so on until the whole court has been covered.

drill 3 *horse and jockey*

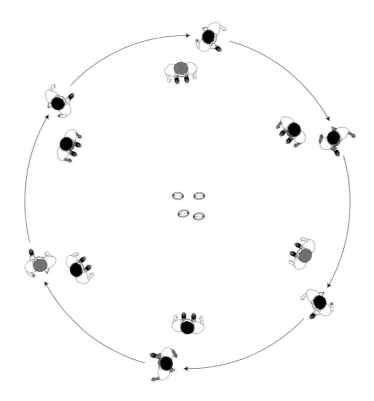

Objective: To warm up the body.

Equipment: Several balls.

Description: Arrange the players into two circles, one inside the other. A number of balls are placed in the middle of the inner circle. On the call of 'left' or 'right' the players in the outside circle have to run in that direction around the entire circle. Once the players get back to their starting position they must go through the legs of a player in the inner circle, grab a ball and return to their start position. Players need to be on their feet before going for a ball. The idea is that there are less balls than there are players to grab them.

Coaching points: Ensure plenty of rest between goes. This will ensure that the players practise high-quality speed and agility over a short distance.

drill 4 *zigzag shuttles*

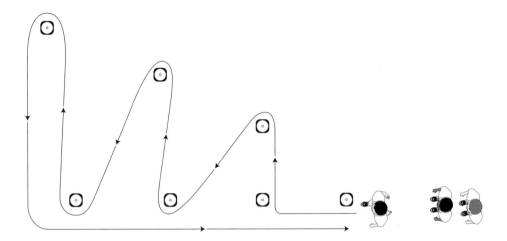

Objective: To warm up by practising sprinting and changing direction.

Equipment: Seven cones and four balls.

Description: Set out the cones as shown above, with the first cone positioned on the corner of the try line and touchline. Players line up off up the touchline from behind this cone. On the coach's command, the first player jogs up to the second cone, turns sharply and sprints to the third cone, turns and jogs up to the fourth cone and so on through the grid as shown, before rejoining the back of the line and waiting his turn to go again. Every player should run holding a ball with both hands in front of the body.

Coaching points: Focus on the need to step sharply off the outside foot to change direction – keep the distances between cones short (maximum five strides). When driving for acceleration, the players should feel themselves lean slightly forwards and take smaller strides. Let the first runner get through two cones before the next runner sets off. Keep the groups large enough that each runner has a good long recovery, but small enough that they do not get cold.

Progression: Ask the runner to start with the ball in two hands and shift it to one hand at each change of direction. The ball should always be on the inside arm (as if the runner is fending off a would-be tackler coming in from the outside). Return the ball to two hands during the jog phases.

drill 5 *snakes*

Objective: To warm up and have fun.

Equipment: One football per team.

Description: Divide the group into teams with a maximum of six players per team. Each team lines up one behind the other, 1 m apart with legs apart.

Player A is the last player in the line and has the ball. On the coach's command, A rolls the ball through the legs of the players in the line, then races to take up position at the head of the line and catch his own roll. Once in possession of the ball and still facing forwards, he picks up the ball and twists his trunk to pass the ball to the player behind, who takes the ball two handed and twists the opposite way to the next player. This left/right twisting motion is repeated until the ball is back with the player at the back of the line, who starts the drill again by rolling the ball through the tunnel of legs once more. Repeat until all players have rolled.

Coaching points: While this is a 'young' drill, the twisting motion is a great warm up for the upper body, and with the two teams racing each other it can be a lot of fun.

drill 6 *dodge tag*

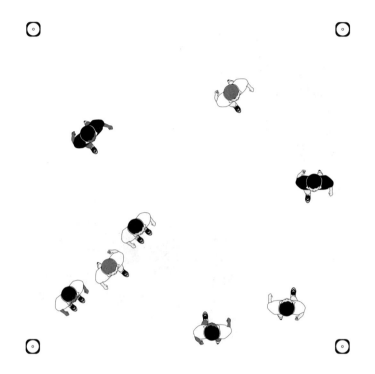

Objective: To practise dodging skills and improve balanced movement.

Equipment: Players.

Description: The playing area selected should be sufficient to allow the number of players to run around but not so large that it allows full freedom of movement. Ideally you should aim to have eight players in a 10 m square area. Use cones to mark the area. Two players are taggers (T). The rest of the players must dodge out of their way and avoid being tagged. Players who have been tagged must stand still, creating barriers for the other players to dodge around.

Coaching points: Encourage players to make a definite dodge move to avoid the obstacles. Look for quick changes of direction, pushing off the outside foot and using hips and shoulders to help keep balanced. All footwork should be balanced and controlled.

Progression: Reduce the size of the playing area and increase the number of taggers.

drill 7 *crazy groups*

Objective: To warm up and encourage concentration.

Equipment: Players.

Description: On the coach's command the players must form groups as per the instruction. For example, if the coach calls 'Fours!' the players must form groups of four, all holding hands with each other and so on.

Coaching points: Once the players have grasped the principle of this drill it can be introduced unexpectedly (with a forfeit for the last group) into any part of the session, just to keep everyone on their toes. This is meant to be fun so don't make the forfeits too arduous!

Progression: Add four cones around the perimeter of the working area. Each cone is given a letter, A–D. On the coach's command all the players have to run around the designated cone before forming into their groups.

drill 8 *reverse wrestling*

Objective: A controlled contact warm up.

Equipment: Players.

Description: Assign players into pairs, and lie face down top-to-toe. On the coach's command, it's a straight race to see who can stand up first. Encourage players to stop their opponent in any way that is permitted within the rules of rugby (strictly no punching, kicking or gouging).

Coaching points: Try, wherever possible, to match up players by size.

SPEED DEVELOPMENT

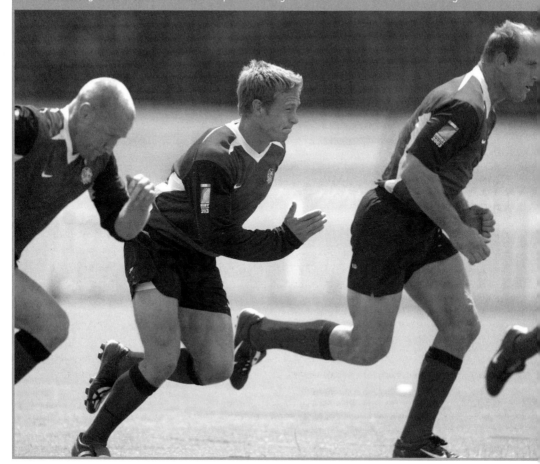

Neil Back, Jonny Wilkinson and Lawrence Dallaglio in sprint training before England's quarter-final match against Wales at World Cup 2003. England went on to win the final against Australia

drill 9 *fast feet*

Objective: To develop foot speed, balance and control of movement.

Equipment: Players.

Description: The players stand on the sideline facing in-field to the 5 m line. Using *very fast* feet and *tiny* steps, the players move towards the 5 m line. When the players reach the 5 m line they turn and walk slowly back to the sideline and start again. The objective is to complete as many tiny steps in the shortest amount of time possible.

Coaching points: Younger children will lose concentration and form very quickly and will increase the length of their steps in order to move forwards more quickly. Re-emphasise the 'fast feet and tiny steps' before each start. The race is not to see who moves forwards fastest, but rather who can get the most steps in over the specified distance.

Progression: Try a timed race – who can perform the most steps in 10 seconds?

drill 10 side jumps

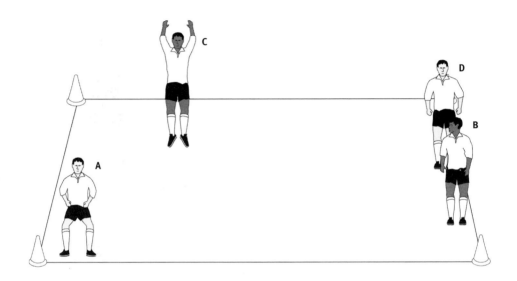

Objective: To improve general agility; to condition the groin muscles (adductors and abductors); to prevent imbalance injuries and stabilise the prime muscle groups.

Equipment: Players.

Description: Split the group into four lines (A, B, C and D), with A and B on one sideline and C and D on the other. All players face up the grid so they are side on to each other. With good posture, line A side-jumps across aiming for height and distance on each jump. Line C then begins the drill, and so on.

Coaching points: Insist on quality at all times. Allow lots of recovery between sets. As players tire there will be a tendency for bodies to sag and for players to twist into a run. Looking backwards to where they came from will help players keep their bodies in the correct position. There is no need for fast forward movements – height and 'hang time' are what you want to see.

Progression: With older players encourage criticism and observation so they become their own coaches. Remind them that form and quality are everything.

drill 11 *high kicks*

Objective: To develop strength and movement skills.

Equipment: Players.

Description: Starting on the sideline, players march out to the centre of the court performing a series of high kicks, clapping their hands under the thigh with each stride. Each leg lift must be as high as possible and the drill must be performed under control. The objective is perfect form, *not speed*.

Coaching points: Insist on straight legs during this movement. Don't allow the body to curl towards the knee. It doesn't matter how high the straight leg comes as long as the form is perfect. Over a period of time the range of movement will improve and develop.

drill 12 *high knees*

Objective: To condition the hip flexors; to learn to lift knees fast and high when running to aid stride length, reduce foot-to-ground contact time and therefore increase speed.

Equipment: Players.

Description: Split the group into four lines (A, B, C and D). A and B stand on one sideline with lines C and D facing them on the other sideline. Line A runs slowly forwards with knees pulled fast and high to the chest, keeping the thighs in line with the direction of running. When they reach the other side, line C begins the drill, then line B and so on. In this way each line has plenty of recovery time.

Coaching points: Insist on quality at all times. Allow lots of recovery time in between sets. As players tire there will be a tendency for bodies to sag and knees to splay outwards. If this happens, stop the players and re-assert the aim to bring the knees up to the chest, not the other way around. There is no need for fast forward motion – foot speed is everything here. Three runs for each group is plenty – mix it in with the other speed drills as part of a post-warm-up.

Progression: With older players, encourage criticism and observation so they become their own coaches. Remember that form and quality are everything.

drill 13 *high skipping*

Objective: To condition the hip flexors, extensors and calf muscles; to teach forceful and short ground contact time in order to develop speed.

Equipment: Players.

Description: Split the group into four lines (A, B, C and D), A and B on one sideline and C and D on the other. With good posture, line A high-skips across the area. When they reach the other line, line C begins the drill and so on.

Coaching points: Insist on quality at all times. Allow lots of recovery between sets. Teach good, tall posture with the top of the head held high. The players should aim for greatest possible height and knee lift, with the front leg raised so that the soles of the shoes are visible to observers in front. Use the arms to assist lift.

Progression: With older players encourage criticism and observation so they become their own coaches. Remind them that form and quality are everything.

drill 14 back to backs

Decelerate/Accelerate   Sprint   Decelerate/Accelerate

Objective: To develop speed and endurance.

Equipment: Four cones.

Description: Mark out a run of 10 m, then 5 m, then 10 m. Players gently accelerate from the first to the second cone, then run flat out for 5 m. They then use the final 10 m to decelerate, turn straight around and start accelerating to the second cone to perform the drill again. There and back is one rep. Each player completes two reps and then walks slowly to fully recover before going again. Start with three sets of two reps and build up slowly over a period of weeks.

Coaching points: Encourage a real change of pace and controlled movement. At the point of acceleration the players should lean forwards slightly, shorten their stride and drive hard back with their elbows.

Progression: Use stopwatches to record times over the middle 5 m. Increase reps by one or two per session while ensuring the quality of the middle section is maintained.

drill 15 *hollow sprints*

Objective: To develop a marked change of pace.

Equipment: Four cones.

Description: Place the cones in a line – the first cone to be placed at 15 m from the touchline, and the remaining three at 5 m intervals. Starting at the touchline, players gently accelerate over the first 15 m to reach full pace at the first marker, hold full pace until the second marker, decelerate to three-quarter pace until the third marker and sharply accelerate to full pace until the last cone. Walk back to the start slowly to recover.

Coaching points: Here the players are training their bodies to go fast, so they need to perform this drill while they are reasonably fresh. You must also allow plenty of rest between sets to ensure that every set is top quality. If you use this drill when players are tired they will never get the feeling of travelling fast.
Tell the players to concentrate on how it feels. When they accelerate, they should drop the hands and lean slightly forwards. This will help to ensure that the power delivered by the legs is propelling the players forwards. Look for changes of speed at the marker point showing control of the pace.

BALL HANDLING
AND ATTACKING

Harlequins' Mel Deane gets a strong pass away as he is tackled in a Quins match against Leeds Tykes in the Zurich Premiership.

drill 16 *ball tag*

Objective: To develop communication skills and speed.

Equipment: Four cones and one ball.

Description: Create a square using the cones (about 5–10 m wide). Three attackers and numerous evaders work within each square, and the objective is for the attackers to tag the evaders with the ball. Once tagged the evader must stand still. The attackers can pass the ball to each other, but once they are in possession they can only pivot on one foot. 'Free' evaders must be aware of stationary 'tagged' evaders, and move and dodge around them.

Coaching points: Encourage lots of communication and movement between attackers, and look for quick but accurate passing.

Progression: Change the attackers regularly and see how many victims they tag in a fixed time (say two minutes).

drill 17 catch-up squares

Objective: To improve passing and movement skills.

Equipment: Four cones and one ball.

Description: Set up a square with the cones about 3 m apart. Player A starts with the ball, and passes to player B. Having given the pass, player A follows it by running to player B and then returning to their starting point. Play continues in this way around the grid.

Coaching points: The key coaching point is to ensure that everyone concentrates on giving a good pass and not just 'unloading' the ball in panic. Remind players that the ball will always travel faster than they do – a valuable lesson in itself!

Progression: When the principle of the drill is mastered, start with an extra ball at the opposite corner. The objective is for one of the balls to catch up with the other, or to play for one minute – whichever comes first.

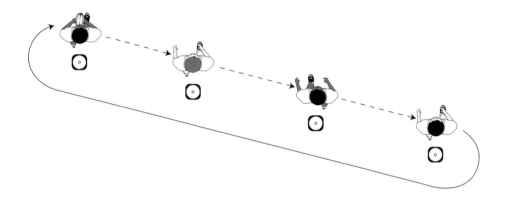

Objective: To introduce basic passing and catching skills.

Equipment: Four cones and one ball.

Description: Place the cones in a gently staggered line, approximately 1.5 m apart. On the coach's command the ball is passed down the line from player to player. When the last player has the ball, he runs around to the first cone, and the rest of the line moves one cone to the right. Play continues until all players have passed at each position. To change the direction of passing, stop the drill and have the players face the opposite direction, so the stagger will be reversed.

When the ball is coming from the left players should stand with their right foot slightly forward, shoulders rotated towards the passer and their hands up ready to receive the ball. Change feet when the ball is coming from the other direction.

Coaching points: The pass should be a smooth movement across the body with a focus on the hands, wrists and arms making the pass, rather than the shoulders.

Progression: Ask the players to run on the spot while completing the same drill.

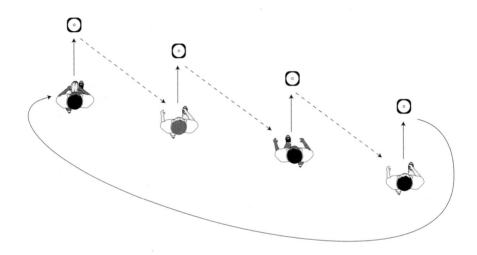

Objective: To introduce passing and catching skills on the move.

Equipment: Four cones and one ball.

Description: Place the cones in a gently staggered line, approximately 1.5 m apart, with each player standing 1 m behind their cone. On the coach's command the first player walks up to his cone and when he reaches it, he passes the ball to the second player, who in turn has walked up to their cone to collect the pass. When the last player has the ball, he runs around to the first cone, and the rest of the line moves one cone to the right. Play continues until all players have passed at each position. To change the direction of passing, stop the drill and have the players face the opposite direction, so the stagger will be reversed.

Coaching points: This simple drill will be a challenge for some younger players as they have to move, think and execute a skill all at once. It is very important they have a clear, concise understanding of the passing and catching skill set – body turned towards the ball and hands up to receive, focus on a spot on the ball to catch and a smooth movement across the body to the receiver.

This drill introduces the concept of timing a walk. Make sure that the walk is at a steady pace so that the catch and pass is completed with a single stride. When the players are resting, talk with them about how they could improve their timing.

drill 20 *passing 3*

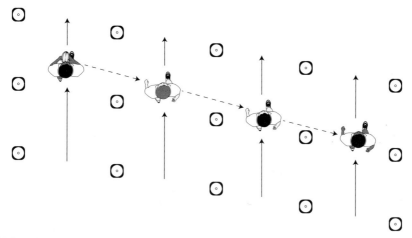

Objective: To develop passing and catching skills on the move.

Equipment: 15 cones and one ball.

Description: Place the cones in a gently staggered line as before. 10 m ahead make another staggered line, with a final line in the centre of the grid. This creates four 'channels' for players to run in. On the coach's command, the first player jogs out and just after the second cone passes to the second player, who in turn has jogged out but remained a few paces behind. The second player then runs for two or three strides before passing to the third player. When the last player has the ball, he runs around to the first cone, and the rest of the line moves one cone to the right. Play continues until all players have passed at each position. To change the direction of passing, stop the drill and have the players face the opposite direction, so the stagger will be reversed.

Coaching points: The catcher must keep a slight distance behind the passer, and be encouraged to run on to the ball. The watchwords are 'run when you have the ball, hold back when you are waiting to receive and then run on to the ball'.

Once a player has passed he must slow down to allow the ball carrier to overtake him. This important concept is at the core of playing rugby – staying behind the ball at all times. As in the previous drills it is very important to continue to re-iterate a clear, concise understanding of the passing and catching skill set. Remind the players what they told you about when they should run, what a well set line looks like etc.

Progression: Increase the speed of running. Once players have mastered the drill you can introduce timed races between groups with penalties for a dropped ball, running out of their channel or a player getting in front of the ball.

drill 21 passing 4

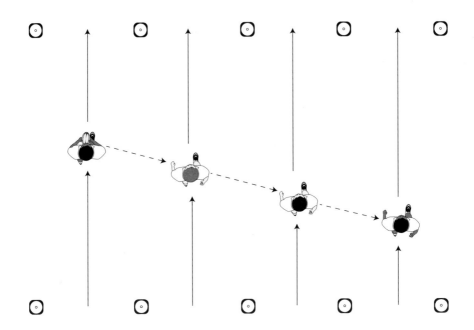

Objective: To improve passing and catching skills on the move.

Equipment: 10 cones and one ball.

Description: Place five cones in a straight line, approx. 2 m apart with another line 15 m opposite. The first player has the ball and on the coach's command he jogs out and passes along the line. When the line reaches the other side of the grid they pause to realign and then return.

Coaching points: The progression from the previous drill is that players do not have a ready-made stagger in the passing line so they must time their run to allow the player with the ball to move ahead.

Progression: Ask players to increase their speed of running. Add a second line to run from the opposite side of the grid at the same time.

moving with the ball

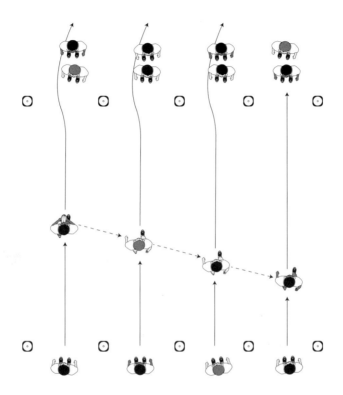

Objective: To introduce handling skills on the move.

Equipment: 10 cones and one ball.

Description: Set up a 10 m square grid with two lines of 5 cones placed 2 m apart. Two players are assigned to stand behind each cone, and the ball is with player 1. On the coach's command, player 1 runs out and passes to player 2, and so forth along the line. When player 4 receives the ball, he continues his run and passes to player 5 who brings his line out and passes as before. The drill continues until all four groups have run.

Coaching points: Players should have their hands up to receive the ball. The ball should move smoothly across the front of the body as they pass, and they must look for the receiver's hands as a target to pass to.

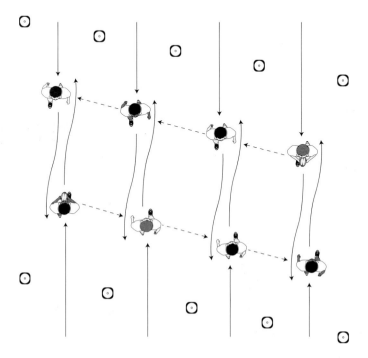

Objective: To improve passing and catching skills on the move.

Equipment: 10 cones and two balls.

Description: Place five cones in a gently staggered line, and make another staggered line 15 m ahead. Players 1 and 5 each have a ball. On the coach's command players 1 and 5 jog out, and pass the ball along their respective lines. When the lines reach the other side of the grid they pause to realign and then return.

Coaching points: This drill requires the players to be even more aware of what is going on around them. There will be a temptation for players to throw the ball away rather than to spot the receiver's hands – the coach can monitor this by watching players' eyes. At some point the players will have to change direction to avoid colliding.

Progression: Ask players to increase their speed of running. If you feel that the players are in control of the drill try removing the stagger from the cones so that runners now have to time their run more accurately. Remind players of what an attacking line looks like and how they should delay their run to allow the staggered formation.

drill 24 *fast hands*

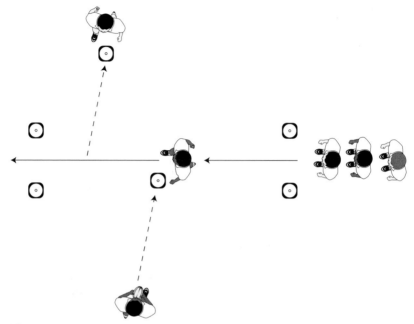

Objective: To develop the ability to give and take a pass quickly.

Equipment: Five cones and one ball.

Description: Place the cones as shown in the diagram. The distance between players F and R depends on their experience. Start with 3 m – it can always be increased. The first player jogs out from the starting position. Upon reaching the central cone he is fed a pass by player F and passes it on to player R. He finishes by running between the final two cones, and then rejoins the back of the line ready to repeat. Keep rotating the players and keep groups small so that there is not too much waiting time. Change the direction of running to practise passing off the other hand.

Coaching points: There will be a tendency for players to drift away from the pass, so encourage the players to run straight. Make sure they run with their hands up ready to receive the pass with their palms facing the passer, and look at the ball as they catch it. The ball should move smoothly across the front of the body as they pass, and they must look for the receiver's hands as a target to pass to.

Progression: Increase the running speed and then reduce the distance between F and R to reduce the time in which to make the pass. As confidence grows, ask player R to alternate between open hands and closed fists. The runner can only pass to open hands, and so *must* look at the receiver. If the runner sees fists he holds the ball and runs hard through the final two cones.

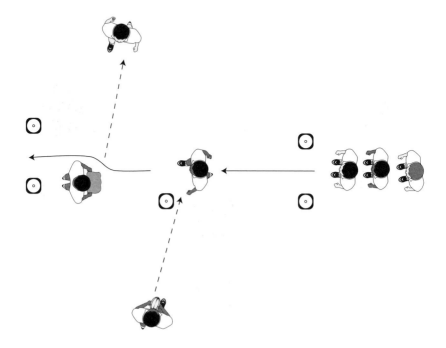

Objective: To improve the ability to give and take a pass quickly.

Equipment: Five cones, one ball and one tackle shield.

Description: Set up the cones as in the previous drill. As before, the first player jogs out from the starting position. Upon reaching the central cone he is fed a pass by player F and passes it on to player R. He finishes by running between the final two cones, and then rejoins the back of the line ready to repeat. The progression in this drill comes from the addition of a player with a tackle shield (player D) who steps up to pressurise the pass. Change the direction of running to practise passing off the other hand.

Coaching points: There will be an even greater tendency for players to drift away from the pass as the pressure comes on from the shield, so remind players to run straight. The runner should continue to focus on the ball and the receiver at all times but should get a feel for checking slightly as the pass is made.

Progression: Initially the shield is only there as a passive obstacle. As skills develop, the player with the shield can take a step towards the runner to increase the pressure.

drill 26 *impossibility*

Objective: To improve passing under pressure – for experienced players.

Equipment: Two balls for every 10 players.

Description: Form a staggered line with 10 players. Players A and B start with a ball. Player B throws his ball straight up above his head, and at the moment the ball leaves his hands, player A passes his ball to B who then passes to C while his original ball is still in the air. The moment player B recovers his original ball he passes to player C who in turn has thrown his ball straight up above his head to free his hands for the receive and pass. Players continue in this way down the staggered line, with player C passing to player D, and so on.

Coaching points: This drill requires a controlled vertical throw and lots of concentration. Player A must take the cue to pass from B's vertical throw. The pass must come in the moment the ball starts its upward path. Introduce it in five-minute blocks each session to avoid players becoming frustrated.

Progression: Race two teams over a set distance, with A running to the end of the line after passing.

drill 27 pick and flick

Objective: To develop a flicked pass from the floor while on the move.

Equipment: Two cones and one ball per team.

Description: Divide the players into teams of no more than four. The two cones (A and B) are set 5 m apart. The ball is placed 2 m in front of cone A. Player 1 runs out and passes the ball from the floor to player 2 who is standing behind cone A, before running through to join the back of the line opposite. Player 2 now places the ball 2 m in front of cone B and runs through to join the back of the line opposite. Player 3 now runs out and passes the ball from the floor to player 4, and so the drill continues.

Coaching points: When introducing the drill, allow the players to move towards the ball at a brisk walk – positioning of the feet is vital and correct technique must be emphasised above speed. When picking the ball up, the rear foot should be beside the ball and the front foot towards the target receiver. The movement is to 'sweep' the ball from the floor rather than to pick it up and then pass. Players should bend the knees rather than the back, as this will allow them to keep their head up and spot the target. Receivers always provide a target with hands up ready.

Progression: Increase the distances slightly.

drill 28 *pick and pass*

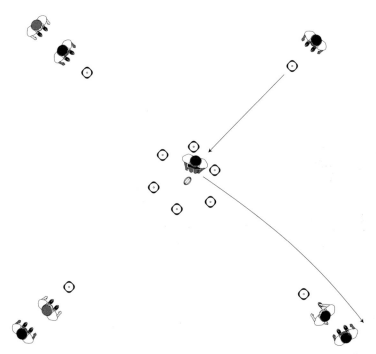

Objective: To develop a pass from the floor while on the move.

Equipment: 10 cones and one ball.

Description: Place six cones in a 1 m diameter circle. Place another four cones 3 m away, as shown in the diagram, with a maximum of three players assigned to each of these cones. Each outer cone is numbered 1–4, and the ball is placed in the centre circle. When the coach calls a number and a direction (e.g. 'one-left'), the first player from the designated cone runs out and passes the ball from the floor in the direction indicated, before running through to join the back of the line directly opposite. The receiver then runs out and places the ball in the circle, before running through and joining the rear of the line opposite. The coach then calls out another number and direction, and so the drill continues.

Coaching points: As before, when picking the ball up the front foot should be beside the ball and towards the target receiver. The movement is to 'sweep' the ball from the floor rather than to pick it up and then pass. Players should bend the knees rather than the back, as this will allow them to keep their head up and spot the target. Receivers always provide a target with hands up ready. The coach must make it clear that as players move around the grid their number will change accordingly.

drill 29 *attacking from broken play*

Objective: To structure an attacking line from a broken play situation.

Equipment: 12 cones and one ball for every 4 players.

Description: Place the cones in lines, with each cone 1 m apart and each line of cones 2 m from the next, as shown in the diagram. Players start as a group at cone X with a ball at cone Y. Each player is given a number 1–4. To start the drill the coach calls a number. The player called becomes the scrum-half and runs to the ball ready to feed the first player. At the same time all the other players run around cone Y and turn to attack up the grid. The drill is complete when the ball reaches the far end of the grid.

Coaching points: This drill requires the players to time their run to ensure that they are in a position to run onto the ball. The cones create channels for each player to run in. The players must run the corner hard so they are facing up the grid and not across it. There is a tendency for players to drift away from the ball and across the grid. A drift is usually a sign that the players are either:

- not timing their run and are forced to move sideways to avoid overrunning the pass or;
- not running the corner hard enough and therefore entering the grid running laterally.

Progression: Ask the players to start by walking in a tight circle around cone X. On the coach's command they must start to run. As there is no designated scrum-half, a player must call for the ball and all other players must communicate with each other to say who has which channel.

drill 30 *combination skills*

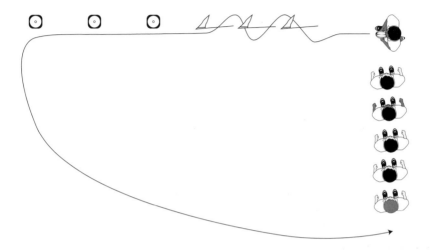

Objective: To introduce a variety of handling skills in a competitive environment.

Equipment: Three cones, three flags and a ball per team.

Description: Split the players into teams of five, and set out the drill area for each team as shown. On the coach's command, each team sets off with the first player carrying the ball, running in and out of the flags. When the ball carrier reaches cone A he places the ball firmly on the floor (as if scoring a try) and runs on to cone B to form the opposition. The second player in line scoops up the try, and makes contact with the opposition on cone B. He hits and falls using the count of three (one = hit, two = down, three = lay back the ball.) The third player then picks up the lay back ball and races to cone C where he simulates a tackle and goes down, protecting the ball. Rolling onto his back he delivers a pop pass to the fourth player who runs past and gives a pass to the fifth player. They then return to the start.

Coaching points: Identify with the players the skills involved; protecting the ball, looking at the ball, using both hands where possible. Timing is vital – if supporting players are too early the line stutters and loses its speed, so they must learn to be slightly late if anything. This will add to the speed of the ball and create a smooth flow of play.

Progression: Hold competitions – which team can do three circuits without a mistake? Which team is the fastest over one, two or three circuits. Pressure is important.

drill 31 *stepping 1*

Objective: To introduce side-stepping skills.

Equipment: Four cones and two balls per team.

Description: Divide the players into teams of six. Place the cones as shown, with the two centre cones 1 m apart. Half the team lines up behind cone A, and the other half lines up behind cone D. On the coach's command, the first players from each team run with the ball towards each other. When they reach the centre cones the players step sharply to their right and then straighten-up to run through to the next player in line. Change to a step to the left when all players have had a turn.

Coaching points: Make sure that both players run straight, and that there is a definite change of direction by pushing off hard on the appropriate leg.

Progression: As confidence grows, decrease the space between the centre cones and increase speed.

drill 32 *stepping 2*

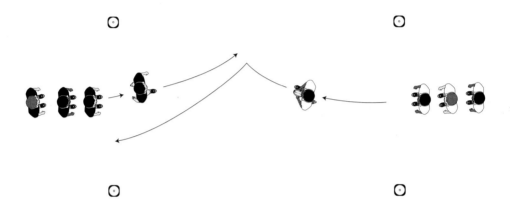

Objective: To develop side-stepping skills.

Equipment: Four cones and one ball per team.

Description: Place the cones as shown, forming a rectangle 5 m x 10 m. Split the players into teams of four. Two teams line up opposite each other at either end of the grid. On the coach's command, player 1 jogs out with the ball in an arc to the right to draw player 2 across the grid. Just before player 1 reaches player 2, he steps sharply to the left and then on to the end of the grid where he passes to player 3 who becomes the attacker, and so the drill continues.

Coaching points: The successful side-step uses the eyes and head as much as anything else. The attacker must 'sell' his intention to go to the right before planting and driving off his right foot. Players can use this drill to experiment how far they need to draw the defender in and across before they step. This drill can also form the start of the defensive skill by showing how the defender can guard against a side-step by staying on the inside shoulder and forcing the ball carrier towards the edge of the grid – the touchline.

Progression: As skills develop, players should gradually increase speed.

drill 33 *fixing a defender – two on one*

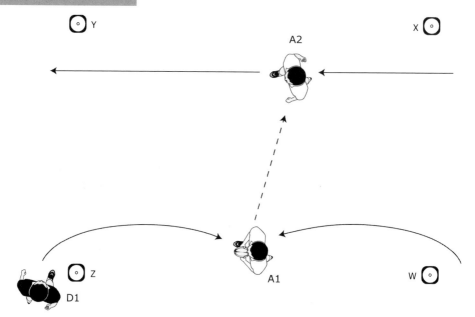

Objective: To teach players how to hold a defender to make space for an attacking team-mate; to time a pass.

Equipment: Four cones and one ball for every team.

Description: Divide the players into teams of four. Place the cones as shown, creating a 5 m by 10 m grid. The attacking player A1 has the ball on cone W and the defending player D1 is on cone Z. Player A2 stands between cones X and Y. On the coach's command, the players enter the grid. The objective for A1 is to make the defender stand still (to 'fix' them) and time a pass to A2 for him to score at the far end of the grid. The defender aims to tag tackle or block the pass.

Coaching points: This is a progression from the previous drill so it is important to carry over the learning. The attacker must run straight at (or slightly to the inside shoulder of) the defender. Any drift will allow the defender to track across and run the attacker out of space against the far boundary of the grid. A2 must time his run relative to A1 to ensure that he takes the ball at close to full speed, travelling straight. After a few runs the defenders may get wise, and now the attacker must run out slightly to create space on both sides of the defender before straightening up and 'fixing'.

Progression: Introduce some competition – 3 points for a score by A2, 1 point for a score by A1, 5 points deducted for a successful defence.

passing out of a tackle

Objective: To introduce the skills required to pass out of a tackle to a supporting player.

Equipment: Four cones, one ball per team and target stickers.

Description: Divide the players into teams of three (ball carrier = C; support runner = S; defender = D) and place target stickers on the thighs of each player. Place the cones as shown, creating a 5 m by 10 m grid. Groups line up one behind the other – players C and S at one end, and D at the other. On the coach's command, player C walks briskly down the centre of the grid with the ball, and player D moves to meet him. As he approaches player D he arcs out slightly to the left to ensure that the tackle is more from the side. As D comes in to tackle, C reaches through the tackle and pops a pass up to S who is running just to the left of the tackler. Repeat the drill with all players rotating starting positions, and ensuring that passes to the left and right are completed.

Coaching points: It is important that the ball carriers get the feeling of moving the defender with the angle of their run so that they can free up enough space to pass through the tackle. The supporting runner must run close to the tackle and must time the run correctly.

Progression: As skills develop, players should gradually increase speed.

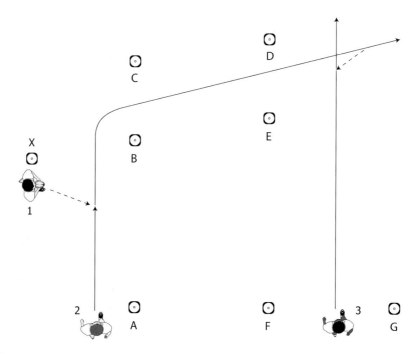

Objective: To introduce players to the scissor move.

Equipment: Eight cones and one ball per team.

Description: Divide the players into teams of three. Place the cones as shown in the diagram. Player 1 has the ball at cone X, player 2 stands to the left of cone A and player 3 stands to the right of cone F. On the coach's command, player 2 runs out to receive a pass from player 1, and then runs on to cone B where he cuts across field using the channel made by cones B-C and D-E. Player 3 runs straight ahead to take the scissor pass on the inside of player 2.

Coaching points: The channel is put in place to force the ball carrier to execute a definite change of direction, and prevent them from running a 'lazy' arc. The principle of this move is to draw defenders out of position – player 2 must first 'interest' the defender by running forwards and then changing direction, causing the defender to come with him. The reverse, or scissor pass, sends player 3 into the resulting gap. Timing is everything – this drill allows players to experiment with how late they can leave a run and what happens if they crowd the pass.

Progression: Remove the cones, and see if the lines of running alter. The most common effect is that players immediately drift rather than running up and then across in a definite change of direction.

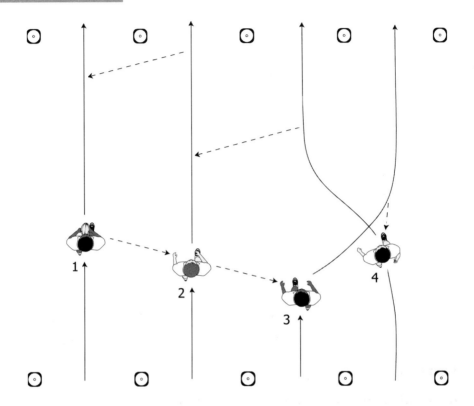

Objective: To develop the scissor move.

Equipment: 10 cones and one ball per team.

Description: Set up cones into eight gates as shown. On the coach's command, player 1 runs out and the ball is passed to player 2 and player 3 in turn. Player 3 now cuts across field and player 4 runs to take the scissor pass on the inside of player 3. Player 4 then passes the ball back to player 2, who in turn passes it back to player 1. The team finishes by running through the gates at the far side of the grid. Change positions and repeat the drill.

Coaching points: Watch the timing of player 4, as there will be a tendency to anticipate the move and the player may have to slow down to take the pass.

Progression: Once the players have mastered this skill, ask them to complete a scissor on the return pass – player 4 passes to player 2 who cuts across player 1 and takes the scissor pass.

drill 37 *run-around or loop*

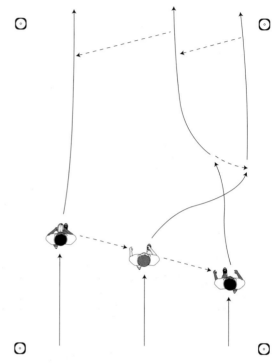

Objective: To introduce the run-around or loop pass.

Equipment: Four cones and one ball per team.

Description: Place the cones as shown, creating a 5 m by 8 m grid. Divide the players into teams of three, and ask them to line up in an attacking line, with player 1 in possession of the ball on the left hand side of the grid. Player 1 runs out and makes a pass to player 2 who in turn passes to player 3. Player 2 now runs around behind to take a short pass on the right of player 3. All players run through to the end of the grid.

Coaching points: When performed accurately, this simple skill is very difficult to defend against, and it is important that the coach is constantly on the lookout for good form:

- player 3 must run dead straight to fix the defender.
- player 2 must run the corner tight to player 3 and turn straight upfield, *not* drift out to take the pass on an angle.

Progression: By introducing a fourth player to the line, player 2 is forced not to drift, as he will end up crowding player 4's space.

CONTACT SKILLS

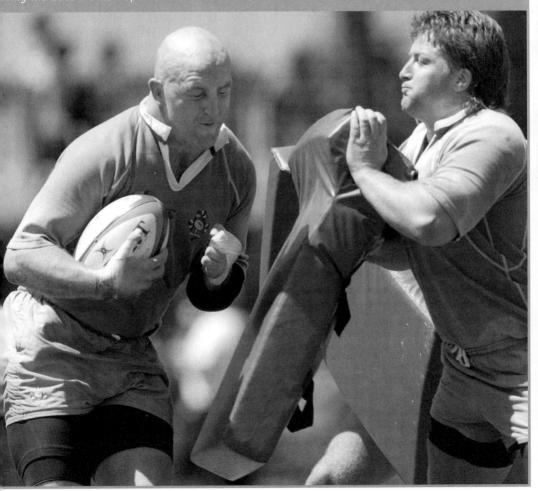

eland legend Keith Wood (with the ball) and Shayne Byrne work with a tackle shield in training
ıring the 2003 World Cup.

drill 38 using the tackle shield 1

Objective: To develop safe and efficient skills when using a tackle shield.

Equipment: Two tackle shields per four or six players.

Description: The player inserts their left arm into the two cross loops of the shield with the right arm supporting the bottom of the shield. The left shoulder is braced to the shield ready to accept contact (for a left handed player the same instructions apply for the right side). The shield carrier leans into the shield with a wide stance side-on so that the weight is over the front left foot. The coach can test the stability of shield carriers by shaking/pushing them. Players with shields face each other, place the face of the shields together and attempt to push the other player backwards. Change shield users and repeat until all players in a team have had a go.

Coaching points: Emphasise the foot positions and the lean into the shield. The shield carriers must understand that they play an important role in any exercise. They must offer a firm, strong platform against which another player can work. The shield must always be kept up vertically, unless otherwise instructed. Shield carriers must absorb every blow, but must not be aggressive.

Progression: Ask players to alternate arms and body positioning when using the shield.

drill 39 using the tackle shield 2

Objective: To develop safe and efficient skills when using a tackle shield.

Equipment: One tackle shield between two players.

Description: Player 1 stands with a tackle shield as described in the previous drill, ready to take contact. Player 2 is kneeling on one knee 2 m from the pad. On the coach's command, player 2 gets up and drives into the pad in an attempt to move it back by 1 m. Stop the drive after a count of three. The shields must put up good resistance and try to hold their ground. Rotate the players so they all get the chance to use the tackle shield, and also be the driver.

Coaching points: By positioning player 2 too close to the shield, there will only be a relatively small amount of momentum from the driving player – this is important whilst the players gain confidence. Insist on good form – players must resist the temptation to bowl into the pad without any control. Shield carriers must absorb every blow, but must not be aggressive. Player 2 must aim to make contact with the shoulder point, and wrap their arms around the pad.

Progression: Change contact shoulder.

drill 40 taking contact with a ball

Objective: To develop the correct contact technique for a ball carrier.

Equipment: One tackle shield and one ball for every two players.

Description: Player 1 stands with a tackle shield as described in the previous drill, ready to take contact. Player 2 stands 2 m from the shield with a ball. On the coach's command player 2 walks into the shield, keeping the ball away from the shield. If contact is made with the left shoulder, the ball should be under the right arm but secured with the left, and vice versa. Player 1 must put up good resistance and try to hold their ground.

Coaching points: The ball carrier must take the ball in two hands but close to the body. Emphasise the correct body position – the cues are as follows:

- ball away from the shield
- head up – aim for a spot on the shield to hit
- hit with the shoulder
- low hips at the point of contact and drive up and forwards and not down.
- use small steps.

At the point of contact have the player shout 'one, two, three' as they drive. They should aim to get two small driving steps in to every count. The shouting helps inject some energy and controlled aggression to the drill. Rotate the players so they all get the chance to use the tackle shield, and also be the driver.

Progression: As competency increases, increase the speed of the ball carrier but do not allow the ball carrier to run more than three strides into the shield. Change contact shoulder.

drill 41 taking contact with a ball and a supporting player 1

Objective: To develop correct contact technique for a ball carrier.

Equipment: One tackle shield and one ball for every three players.

Description: Player 1 stands with a tackle shield as described in the previous drill, ready to take contact. Player 2 stands 2 m from the pad with a ball. On the coach's command, player 2 walks into the pad keeping the ball away from the shield. Player 1 must put up good resistance and try to hold their ground. Player 3 acts as the supporting player – as player 2 makes contact player 3 follows in to secure the ball. Rotate the players so they all get the chance to use the tackle shield, and also be the driver and supporter.

Coaching points: The ball carrier must take the ball in two hands but close to the body. Player 3 must watch which way player 2 hits the shield – if it is with the left shoulder then player 3 should drive in on the ball using his right, protecting the ball from the side. This sounds complex, but it will become the obvious way for player 3 to hide or shield the ball. If he goes in on the wrong shoulder then he cannot make contact with his shoulder as player 2's backside will be in the way and the ball will be there for all to see.

Progression: As competency increases, increase the speed of the ball carrier but do not allow the ball carrier to run more than three strides into the shield. Shield carriers must provide a strong target and absorb the impact, but must not be aggressive.

taking contact with a ball and a supporting player 2

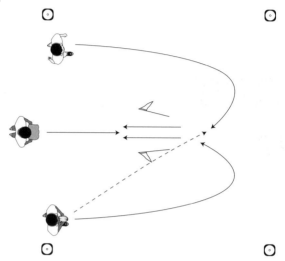

Objective: To improve contact technique for a ball carrier and supporting players; to introduce the concept of offside for a supporting player joining a contact situation.

Equipment: One tackle shield, one ball, two corner flags and four cones for every three players.

Description: Place the cones (A, B, C, D) as shown in the diagram, creating a 3 m by 4 m grid, with two corner flags 1 m infield and 1 m apart forming a 'gate'. Player 1 stands between cones A and B with a tackle shield, ready to take contact. Player 2 (with the ball) and player 3 stand beside player 1, with all three players facing the same direction into the grid. Player 2 rolls the ball out between the flags and player 3 runs to gather the ball before turning to make contact with the pad through the gate. Player 2 runs out with him and turns to act as the supporting player. Both players must go out on the outside of the flags and return through the gate. The shield must put up good resistance and try to hold their ground. Rotate the players so they all get the chance to use the tackle shield, and also be the driver and supporter.

Coaching points: Ensure that the ball is rolled within the grid, therefore restricting the distance the ball carrier can run into the shield. The supporting player must return through the 'gate', ensuring they come from an onside position to join the contact (the idea of a gate at the back of a maul or ruck is one that is often used by referees to indicate where players can join). Ensure that there is good ball protection on impact, and that the supporting player binds with the ball carrier.

drill 43 ball retention on contact

Objective: To accustom players to retain possession of the ball when in contact and going to ground.

Equipment: Two cones, one shield and one ball for every group.

Description: Divide the players into groups of three, four or five. Place the cones 3 m apart. One player stands at cone B with the shield, while the rest of the players stand at cone A in a line. On the coach's command, the first player advances to the shield and gives a loud count of 'one' (drives into the shield), 'two' (drops to the ground protecting the ball), 'three' (lays the ball back with both hands, under control). The player then returns to the team with the ball, which is handed to the next player and the drill is repeated.

Coaching points: The contact must be firm, positive and vigorous. Shield holders must be encouraged to play their part to make a firm base. As the player contacts the shield, the ball must be kept away from the shield, and it must not touch it. When the player falls, the ball must not touch the ground, until it is laid back under complete control.

Progression: A team drill can be developed, with a second player running out as the ball is presented on the count of three, picking it up and running around the shield before returning to the next player to continue.

drill 44 *controlling the ball on impact*

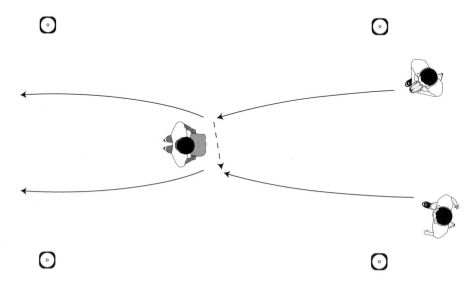

Objective: To develop the correct technique when establishing a ruck.

Equipment: One tackle shield, one ball and four cones for every three players.

Description: Place the cones (A, B, C, D) as shown in the diagram, creating a 3 m by 4 m grid. Player 1 stands in the centre of the grid with a tackle shield, ready to take contact. Players 2 and 3 are at the end of the grid between cones A and B with the ball on the floor just in front of them. On the coach's command, player 2 gathers the ball and then drives into the shield in an attempt to move it back 1 m. After contact, player 2 falls to the floor keeping the ball close and secure, before pushing it out along the floor at arms length allowing player 3 to pick up and run through to the far cones (C and D) to be joined by player 2. The ball is placed on the floor again, and the drill is repeated with player 3 carrying. Keep rotating the players so they all get a chance to play in the different positions.

Coaching points: Ball carriers must fall with their back to the shield. There must be a defined structure to this process, and you might find it helpful to illustrate this by walking the players through the drill and applying a key word to each phase such as 'hit, drive, down, ball'. There will be a tendency for younger players to flop on the floor and just release the ball. Encourage the players to focus on controlling the ball at all times. Praise players who do not let the ball touch the floor before it is placed back. Players can call out 'hit, drive, down, ball' to help focus.

clearing out at the tackle

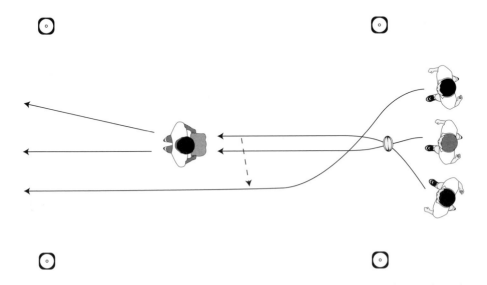

Objective: To develop the correct technique when clearing defenders from a tackle situation.

Equipment: One tackle shield, one ball and four cones for every four players.

Description: Place the cones (A, B, C, D) as shown in the diagram, creating a 3 m by 5 m grid. Player 1 stands in the centre of the grid with a tackle shield, ready to take contact. Players 2, 3 and 4 are at the end of the grid between cones A and B, with the ball on the floor just in front of them. On the coach's command, player 2 gathers the ball and then drives into the shield in an attempt to move it back 1 m. As before, player 2 falls to the floor after contact, keeping the ball close and secure. Player 3 steps over player 2 and drives into the shield to clear the tackle area. The ball is then pushed back for player 4 who comes in to pick up the ball and runs through to the far cones (C and D). The ball is placed on the floor again, and the drill is repeated with player 3 carrying. Keep rotating the players so they all get a chance to play in the different positions.

Coaching points: Timing is everything. If player 3 is too late the ball will be lost too soon and the ball carrier will not have gone to ground and there will not be a target to hit. Players 2 and 3 must quickly get away from the contact to support player 4.

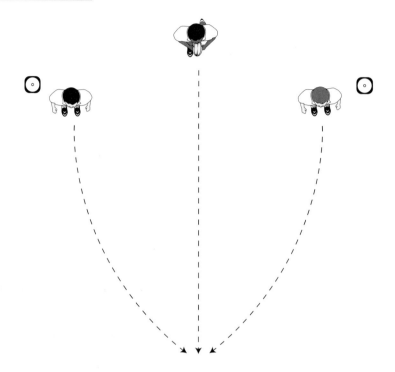

Objective: To develop competition for a loose ball on the floor.

Equipment: Two cones and one ball for every three players.

Description: Place the two cones 1 m apart, with players 1 and 2 positioned on the inside of each of them. Player 3 has the ball. On the coach's command, player 3 rolls the ball between the two players (no more than 3 m). The moment the ball hits the floor, players 1 and 2 compete to secure the ball. Assume that players 1 and 2 are playing in the direction of the arrows. This will help in understanding which way to fall. Each player will try to fall with his back to the arrow.

Coaching points: Try, wherever possible, to match up players by size. Encourage the players to fall hard on the ball, and to position their body between the opposition and the ball. In this way they will be presenting the ball to players who, in a game, will be coming to support. Ball speed and controlled aggression are the keys to success, but do not allow any more wrestling on the ground than would be allowed in a game. The player arriving second is not allowed to fall on the player in possession, but can compete for the ball as long as he stays on his feet.

drill 47 clearing out the tackle – game situation

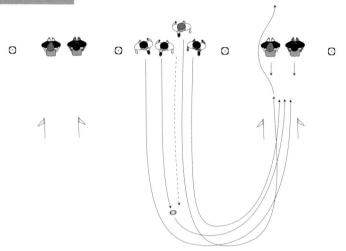

Objective: To simulate clearing defenders from a tackle situation.

Equipment: Four tackle shields, one ball, four corner flags and four cones for every eight players.

Description: Place the cones (A, B, C, D) at 2 m intervals in a line. Four players have tackle shields, and they are set up in tight pairs between cones A/B and C/D with a pair of flags 1 m apart and 1 m in front of each pair to make an 'onside gate'. The remaining players 1–4 stand between cones B/C. The ball is rolled out (no more than 4 m) and player 1 runs out to gather it before turning and driving into one pair of shields (his choice) via a gate, and goes to floor to present the ball as before. As the ball is rolled out, the shields advance one stride to just behind the gates. Players 2 and 3 bind together and drive them out of the way. Player 4 follows up to secure the ball and runs through to complete the drill. Allow plenty of rest and keep rotating the players.

Coaching points: Before the drill starts, emphasise the key points for the shield holders and driving/clearing players. The shields must put up good resistance and try to hold their ground on impact. Ball carriers must fall with their back to the shield. Walk each group through perfect form so that everyone understands before increasing pace. Timing of the arrival at the clearout is vital. Too soon and there is no momentum. Too late and the ball will be lost.

Progression: When competency is established allow more freedom amongst the attackers. Communication is key to the success of this – one player must call for the ball and supporters must talk so everyone knows their role within the drill.

drill 48 competing for the ball on the floor – group skills

Objective: To develop group competition skills for a loose ball on the floor.

Equipment: One ball for every six players.

Description: Divide the players into teams of three. Each team of three then pairs up to play against each other. Players line up in their teams, 1 m apart and facing in the same direction (as if in a lineout). The coach stands facing the lines (no more than 3 m away) with the ball. The coach throws the ball straight up to around head height. The moment the ball hits the floor the two groups compete to secure the ball.

Coaching points: Try, wherever possible, to match up players by size. Encourage the players to fall hard on the ball, secure it safely and position their body between the opposition and the ball. In this way they will be presenting the ball to players who, in a game, will be coming to support. Ball speed and controlled aggression are the keys to success, but do not allow any more wrestling on the ground than would be allowed in a game. The player arriving second is not allowed to fall on the player in possession but can compete for the ball as long as he stays on his feet. The player on the floor can pass the ball up to supporters if he is not being tackled, and can also roll it back.

drill 49 clearing out at the tackle – progression

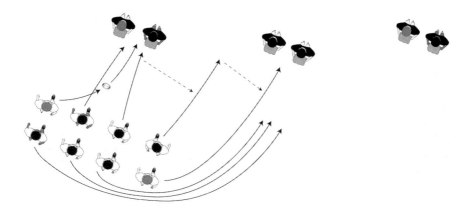

Objective: To improve clearing defenders from a tackle situation.

Equipment: Six tackle shields and one ball for every 14 players.

Description: Six players have tackle shields, and they are set up in tight pairs in a staggered line as shown, no more than 5 m apart. The attackers (players 1–8) stand 3 m in front of the first pair of shields. The coach drops the ball in front of the attackers, one of whom (player 1) picks up and drives into the first pair of shields. The drill develops as follows:

- Players 2 and 3 drive over to clear out the shields
- Player 4 comes in as dummy half and passes to player 5 who drives into the second pair of shields
- Players 6 and 7 drive the shields away
- Player 8 comes in as dummy half and passes to the supporting players arriving from the previous contact, and continues the drill into the final pair of shields.

Allow plenty of rest and keep rotating the players.

Coaching points: This drill requires all players to have a good understanding of the skills involved, and should not be introduced until the previous drills are clearly understood. Walk the players through the drill and slowly increase the speed. Emphasise the need for players to get back into support quickly after contact is made and to get the ball away. Communication is key to the success of this drill, so players must talk to each other often. Timing is critical, particularly for players taking the pass from the dummy half.

drill 50 pop pass from the tackle

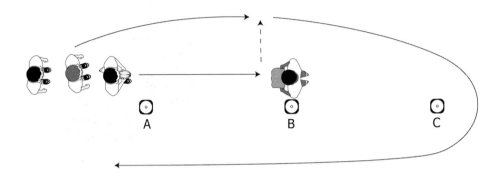

Objective: To introduce the skill of delivering a pop pass from a tackled player on the ground.

Equipment: Three cones, one shield and one ball for every group.

Description: Divide the players into groups of three, four or five. Place the cones in a line, 3 m apart. One player stands at cone B with the shield, while the rest of the players stand at cone A in a line. On the coach's command, the first player runs forwards with the ball, drives into the shield, and falls to the ground protecting the ball. As he falls, the second player from the team runs forwards to his aid. As he arrives, the fallen player on his back delivers a soft upwards pass into the stomach of his oncoming team-mate. The ball is then carried around cone C and back to the team for the drill to be repeated.

Coaching points: The ball must not touch the ground. The tackled player must protect the ball on impact, and must attempt to land on his side, shoulder or back in order to be able to see the oncoming supporter and to deliver the pass. Emphasise that the pass must be careful and delivered accurately into the midriff. On no account must it be a hard pass. The supporting player must time his run, arriving at the pass at maximum speed and carrying on to the next cone.

Progression: When a degree of skill has developed, two players can support the fallen player – one to receive the pop pass and the other to receive a second pass.

drill 51 competitive ball possession

Objective: To accustom young players to compete vigorously but fairly for ball possession.

Equipment: One ball per pair.

Description: Pair up the players, trying to match them by size where possible. These pairs are spread over a teaching area, with one player in possession of the ball. On the coach's command, the other player attempts to wrestle the ball from his partner's grasp. Time the wrestle, starting with 10 seconds. You can increase the time, but do not allow combats to go on too long.

Coaching points: The ball carrier can bend and hide the ball in the midriff. He can also turn away from the tackler, and is allowed to protect his ball vigorously. Body shaking, pushing and even jumping up and down can be permitted under strict controls. The tackler can use any means available under the rules of rugby to win the ball. No hitting is allowed. A useful tip is to drive an arm either up or down between the player's body and the ball.

Progression: When players are used to this exercise, encourage them to push at the same time. The tackler may fight for the ball and at the same time gain ground even though he doesn't win the ball.

LINEOUT

With the aid of their team-mates, South Africa's Juan Smith and Australia's Nathan Sharpe contest a lineout ball in their 2006 Tri-Nations match in Sydney.

throwing-in and catching at a lineout

Objective: To introduce the lineout skill of catching a ball above the head.

Equipment: Four cones and one ball for every five players.

Description: Place the cones in a diamond shape as shown, with the outer cones 5 m from the central cone. Players 1–4 stand at cones A–D with a catcher (C) in the middle. The catcher stands with his arms above his head, and player 1 attempts to hit the catcher's hands using a soccer-style throw-in. The catcher then passes to the next thrower in sequence and the exercise is repeated around the diamond. Then the catcher changes places with the thrower, and the exercise is repeated until all have had a turn at catching.

Coaching points: The catcher should stand with their hands six to eight inches apart, with their palms at about 45-degrees forming a funnel. The emphasis is on relaxed hands – do not grab at the ball. Throwers should experiment with holding the ball across the widest part, or with one hand on the widest part and the other on the rear part.

Progression: On catching the ball, the player turns to the left, pulls the ball down into his waist and bends quickly over the ball to hide it. Try this sequence slowly at first, and as players become more skilful ask them to turn and bend in one movement.

drill 53 *jumping and catching*

5m — P1 — **5m** — P2 — P3

Objective: To develop jumping and catching skills.

Equipment: One ball and three cones for every three players.

Description: Place the cones in a straight line, 5 m apart. One player stands at each cone. Player 1 throws in to player 2, who stands with arms slightly raised. The throw is aimed slightly above the hands of player 2 so that they have to jump to catch it. If the ball goes over player 2, player 3 must catch it, and have a turn at throwing.

Coaching points: The players must have good body positioning with their legs and arms slightly bent. Timing is crucial, and the jump should not be attempted until the ball is in the air. When they catch the ball, the player must land and bend into the ball-protecting position. Rotate the players so that they have all had a turn in each position.

Progression: As specialist jumpers emerge, ask the throwers to test how high the jumper can reach. The ultimate skill is to be able to catch the ball and at the top of the jump using the hands and wrists to flick the ball down to the scrum-half. This is a skill that is rare in young players. It will develop with time, age and experience. Work slowly and carefully on this aspect.

drill 54 *target practice*

Objective: To develop lineout throwing accuracy.

Equipment: One ball and a target set at 6–7 ft high (e.g. the bottom of a basket-ball net, a chalk mark on a wall or a rope hanging with a ribbon tied to it from a crossbar) per team of four.

Description: Divide the players into teams of four. One player is the thrower, and stands at least 5 m from the target. Using a soccer-style throw-in they aim to hit the target. The remaining three players cluster around the target to field the ball and return to thrower.

Coaching points: Ensure the thrower has a good backswing behind the head to propel the ball. Throwing from directly over the head is not efficient.

Progression: Set three cones at varying distances from the target – one at 5 m, 7 m and 9 m so the thrower can practise throwing from varying distances. Note – younger players will not necessarily have the strength to make a 9 m throw.

drill 55 passing off the top of the lineout

Objective: To develop the pass from the lineout to scrum-half.

Equipment: One ball and four cones for every four players.

Description: Place the cones in a square, with a player positioned at each cone. Player 1 throws the ball as in a lineout for player 2 to catch. After catching the ball, player 2, with his hands still above his head, turns and passes to player 3. Player 3 then throws to player 4 who turns and passes to player 1. Repeat around the square.

Coaching points: This is a difficult skill for young players. Emphasise the need to turn slightly before passing. The pass off the top should aim at the target player's raised hands. The pass will inevitably drop in flight, allowing a good catching opportunity. If aimed at the waist the drop in flight can cause the catcher to bend.

Progression: Catcher bends at the waist to protect the ball and then passes to scrum-half.

Objective: To develop a system of protecting the ball after the lineout catch.

Equipment: One ball and two cones for every four players.

Description: Players are set out as shown in the diagram. Allow an arm's length between each member of the lineout team. Player 1 throws to player 3 (with raised arms). Player 3 pulls the ball down into his waist and bends, then players 2 and 4 move in to bind around the waist of player 3 (player 2 with right arm and player 4 with left arm). After completion, players 2, 3 and 4 will form a 'V' shape.

Coaching points: Measuring the distance between themselves and the player in front by using an arm's length will prevent over-crowding. Players 2 and 4 must face player 3 during the throw. On contact, the heads of players 2 and 4 must be at waist level. Emphasise good foot positioning with wide stance, toes pointing forwards, knees bent, chin up, flat back and eyes up and open. The bind must be tight, and the ball must be buried out of sight. Rotate the players so that they have all had a turn in each position.

Progression: Add two players with tackle shields to act as opposition for the maul to push against. Player 1 (the thrower) can follow up to take the ball from the back of the maul.

drill 57 *five man lineout*

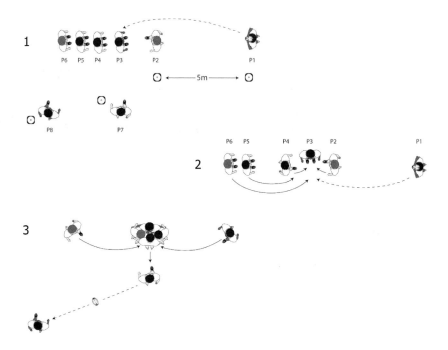

Objective: To develop more player involvement in the lineout.

Equipment: One ball and four cones per team.

Description: Lineout players set out as in diagram. Player 1 is 5 m from the front of the line with the ball. Player 7 is 2 m from the lineout as a scrum-half. Player 8 is 10 m from the line as an outside half. Throw in to P3 who bends and conceals the ball at waist level. P2 and P4 move in and bind to make a V shape. P5 moves in to secure the ball while staying bound with one arm in the pushing position. (This is called 'smuggling'.) P1 and P6 move in and bind onto the two players (P2 and P4) already in position to complete the maul. P7 (the scrum-half) goes into the back of the 'V' between the players to take the ball, which is then passed to P8. Repeat the exercise 3/4 times, then rotate players.

Coaching points: This is a complicated procedure at first. Play it slowly and then speed up. Emphasise good foot positioning with wide stance, toes pointing forwards, knees bent, chin up, flat back and eyes up and open. Emphasis is on a tight bind and a good pushing position at all times.

Progression: One of the players at the back can slip a binding arm and secure the ball from the catcher and present it back to P8.

drill 58 defensive lineout 1

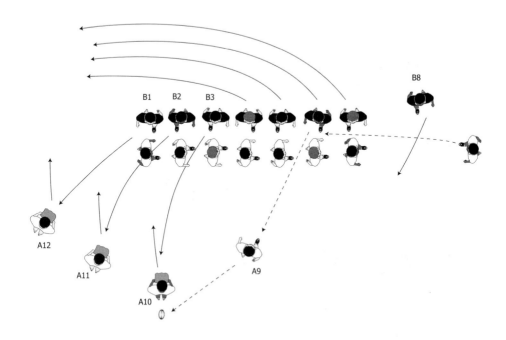

Objective: To develop skills and practices associated with a defensive lineout.

Equipment: One ball, three tackle shields and three cones.

Description: Divide the players into teams, with each team containing two sets of forwards (six or eight aside) and three backs with tackle shields (on the attacking side). The lineout is uncontested and the attacking side wins the ball. It is passed to the scrum-half (A9) who passes slightly behind and as if the ball goes to floor. The drill continues as if the attacking backs are in possession and the ball has been passed to players A10, A11 and A12 who have advanced as if attacking with the ball. The back three defending forwards B1, B2 and B3 leave the lineout and attack the shields in a defensive formation. The defensive hooker (B8) closes around the front of the lineout to block any potential blind side moves by the scrum-half. The remainder of the defensive forwards having determined that the ball is away can support across field. Give each set of forwards a turn.

Coaching points: The defending players must not leave the lineout until the ball has passed from the lineout to the scrum-half. Organisation is needed to allocate defensive roles to the back three players to avoid all three going for the same shield.

drill 59 *defensive lineout 2*

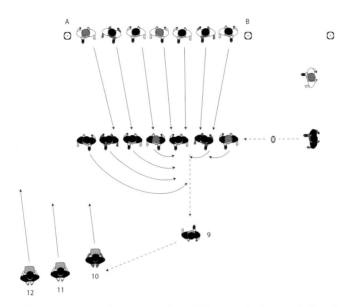

Objective: To accustom players to the skills needed in a defensive lineout.

Equipment: One ball, three tackle shields and four cones.

Description: Divide the players into teams, with each team containing two sets of forwards (six or eight aside), a scrum-half and three backs (on the attacking side). The lineout players must be contained within the two cones A and B, which are 15 metres apart. The lineout is uncontested and the attacking side wins the ball. Immediately players bind in around it to set up a maul to protect the ball and the defending side sets up to defend. No push is required at this stage. The ball is smuggled back to the scrum-half (player 9) who passes slightly behind player 10 and the ball goes to floor. The drill continues as if the attacking backs are in possession and the ball has been passed to player 11 and player 12 who have advanced as if attacking. One or more defending forwards must bind on the side of the maul, looking to the opposition to see what is happening. When the ball is released by player 9 the first defender off the side of the maul heads to mid-field with the intention of getting between player 10 and player 12 to make a tackle and disrupt their line.

Coaching points: The offside law must be observed, players must remain properly bound to the maul, otherwise they must retire behind the back foot of the maul.

Progression: Practise slowly, and gradually increase speed. Begin with an uncontested lineout then graduate to the attacking side being allowed to win the ball but putting in a contested push.

drill 60 *offside from the kicker*

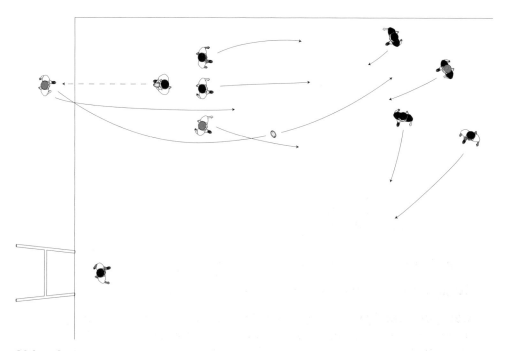

Objective: To emphasise the rules governing being offside in front of the kicker, and to practise procedures.

Equipment: 8, 9 or 10 players – several balls.

Description: Set up three or four players in a lineout complete with scrum-half, and out-half or full-back (kicker). Other players form a reception group 20 m along the touchline. Ball is passed from the lineout to the scrum-half, who passes to the kicker to kick downfield, aiming for touch. Reception group field the ball and start a passing movement back upfield. Lineout forwards move downfield to cut off the impending attack.

Coaching points: Prime objective is to ensure that no lineout player begins a run in front of the kicker before the ball is kicked and he has advanced – emphasise that this is the basis of the offside law. Change players around and test new kickers.

Progression: Lineout forwards do not all attack the reception group's ball-carrier; some fan out across the pitch to cut off passes into mid-field.

RUCK, MAUL, SCRUM

Scotland's Craig Hamilton and Scott Murray lend their weight and power to a scrum in training at Murrayfield.

drill 61 *pushing position 1*

Objective: To introduce young players to the skill of pushing.

Equipment: A wall.

Description: Ask players to place their hands flat against the wall a little below chest height, and move their feet back until the player is at an angle of approx. 45 degrees. The weight should be taken through the hands. Ask players to walk their hands down the wall, bending their knees as they go to achieve a comfortable pushing position with a 'proud' chest and flat back. Count to three to hold the position.

Coaching points: Emphasise good positioning with wide stance, toes pointing forwards, knees bent, chin up, flat back and eyes up and open. Watch out for rounded backs – this is a weak position and needs to be avoided – and emphasise the need for a straight spine. Practise this drill so that players learn to lean into the wall, balancing their weight through their hands. Increase the time held in position, but no more than a count of five.

drill 62 *pushing position 2*

Objective: To develop the skill of pushing.

Equipment: Players.

Description: Divide the players into pairs, and ask them to face each other on hands and knees and bind against each other in a scrummaging position with their toes pushed into the ground. On the coach's command, both players push forwards under control, which will cause them to come up into the pushing position. The position is held for a count of three before they lower back to the starting position. By repeating the movement the players can gain confidence in a controlled environment.

Coaching points: Emphasise the correct body position at all times. It is a good idea to break the movement down into two stages:

1. **squeeze** – the player squeezes everything tight, braces the chest and pulls the belly button in (to protect the back) and pulls the bind tight.
2. **up** – the player pushes back and away, retaining tension in their chest and core, and pushing off the ground with their toes.

Ensure that players don't round their backs as they move off the ground. When introducing this drill allow each player to keep a hand on the ground throughout before progressing to binding with both arms.

Progression: Introduce some competition by allowing the players to push. Don't allow any player to be pushed more than 1.5 m.

drill 63 *pushing position 3*

Objectives: To develop the skill of pushing with a dynamic exercise.

Equipment: One tackle shield for every two players.

Description: Divide the players into pairs. One player holds the shield and the other player adopts the pushing position by wrapping their arms around the shield. Players must walk their legs backwards to achieve the correct position, and hold for a count of three. Players then change position so they both have a chance to use the shield. There should be no forward movement.

Coaching points: Emphasise good positioning with wide stance, toes pointing forwards, knees bent, chin up, flat back and eyes up and open. Watch out for rounded backs – this is a weak position and needs to be avoided – and emphasise the need for a straight spine. Ensure that the shoulder of the pusher is solidly in contact with the shield, and instruct the shield carriers to provide a solid platform against which to push – without this solid platform the pusher will fall down.

Progression: Line up the shields, and stand behind the line of shields providing a hand signal for the pushers to stop. This requires the players to look up.

Objective: To develop the skills together to push in a scrummage.

Equipment: Two tackle shields for every four players and four cones.

Description: Divide the players into two sets of pairs, and place the cones in a 3 m grid. Two players take up tackle shields and stand shoulder-to-shoulder between the top two cones. A second pair of players (pushers) stands facing them between the bottom two cones, shoulder-to-shoulder with their inside arms around each other's waists. Pushers step forwards to the shields and bend into a pushing position – the player on the right puts his head into the gap between the two shields. Their arms should be bound around the shield firmly, and their shoulders are in contact with the shield. On the coach's command, the pushers must attempt to push the shields backwards, but no more than half a metre. Try two or three repetitions, then change shield carriers.

Coaching points: Emphasise the correct body position as shown in the previous three drills. Take this exercise in slow stages and watch carefully how individuals are reacting. Step in quickly if there is any twisting or danger of falling. Pushers must work together as a pair and be firmly bound around each other's waist. Ensure that shield carriers play their part, giving a firm upright stable platform. They should retreat slightly on the push but maintain good pressure on the pushers – they are there to help the players develop good pushing skills, not to drive them back.

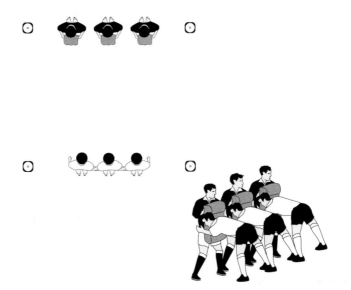

Objective: To develop the skills of a scrum front row.

Equipment: Three tackle shields, four cones and one ball for every six players.

Description: Divide the players into two sets of three, and place the cones in a 3 m grid. Three players take up tackle shields and stand shoulder-to-shoulder between the top two cones. The other three players stand facing them between the bottom two cones, with the two outside players (props) binding around the waist of the middle player (hooker). The hooker binds across the backs/shoulders of the two props, gripping their jerseys. On the coach's command, they step forward to the shields – the middle player puts their head into the left gap between the shields and the right hand player puts their head into the right gap. The shoulders of all three pushers make contact with the shields. Pushers move their feet backwards and hold against the shields. The two outside players bind strongly around the shields. On the 'bend' command they bend knees; on the 'push' command they straighten knees and attempt to push the shields backwards. Repeat two or three times then change players.

Coaching points: Emphasise the correct body position as shown in the previous drills; foot position of players with shields is important, in order to provide pushing players with a strong, continuous base.

drill 66 *front row in contact*

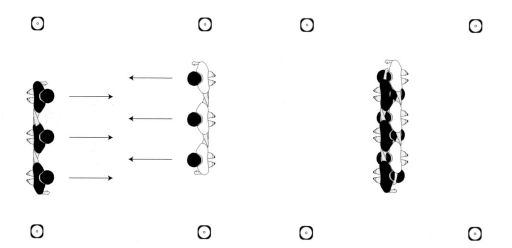

Objective: To develop the skills of two front rows operating in contact.

Equipment: Four cones and one ball for every six players.

Description: Divide the players as shown, inside the cones in a 2 m grid. The players stand in two rows facing each other. Players follow the coach's commands:

- **'crouch'** – both rows bend at the waist (an arm's length apart) and prepare to make contact.
- **'hold'** – they wait
- **'engage'** – they make contact using correct body positions.

(The top row is deemed to have possession of the ball, therefore the heads of the opposition fit into the gaps as shown in the above diagram.)

- **'push'** – the two rows lean on each other for a count of three.
- **'stop'** – the two rows break up.

Repeat slowly three or four times to accustom players to the experience.

Coaching points: Emphasise the correct body position: a wide stance and feet at 45 degrees, the soles of boots on the ground to give better traction. Bend the knees to lower body height, keep chin up, push chest through for a flat back, eyes open looking for the ball. Knees must not come forwards under the body. They must be kept well back to allow the spine to straighten and deliver the push from the knees.

drill 67 the expanded scrummage 1

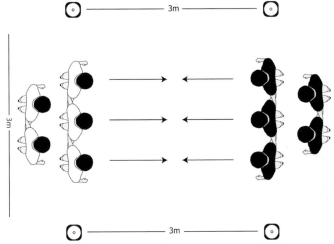

Objective: To develop skills, strength and experience to compete in a five-player scrummage.

Equipment: Four cones and one ball for every 10 players.

Description: Divide the players into two sets of five, and place the cones in a 3 m grid. The players stand in two rows facing each other, with three players at the front and two players behind. Players follow the coach's commands:

- **'bind'** – the front rows bind as in drill 66. The two players behind (the locks) bind around each other's waists.
- **'crouch'** – the front rows bend, the two locks remain standing.
- **'touch'** – the front row extends their arms to contact the opposition.
- **'engage'** – the front rows move forwards and lock into position.
- **'lock'** – the two locks insert their heads into the front row. The locks bind strongly around the buttocks of the players in front.
- **'lean'** – the two scrums lean into each other.

Repeat three of four times, slowly and using the command sequence, to accustom players to the experience.

Coaching Points: Emphasise the correct body position: wide stance and feet at 45 degrees, the soles of boots on the ground to give better traction. Bend the knees to lower body height, keep chin up, push chest through for a flat back, eyes open looking for the ball. Knees must not come forwards under the body. They must be kept well back to straighten spine and deliver the push from the knees.

Binding is a vital part of the process, and its importance must be emphasised. Locks can grab the jersey of their props to generate a strong link.

drill 68 *the expanded scrummage 2*

Objective: To develop skills, strength and experience to compete in a six-player scrummage.

Equipment: Four cones and one ball for every 12 players.

Description: When a degree of confidence and skill has been attained in the five-player scrummage in drill 67, two players can be added (No. 8s) to bind onto the two locks, following the same instructions as in drill 67. Practise in sets of three uncontested scrums to start – then introduce a push when it is felt appropriate.

Coaching Points: The same points are valid for the no. 8s as for the locks and props – a wide stance and feet positioned at 45 degrees. The soles of boots should be on the ground as much as possible to give better traction. Bend the knees to lower body height, keep chin up, push chest through to get a flat back, eyes open looking for the ball. Knees must not come forwards under the body. They must be kept well back to allow the spine to straighten and deliver the push from the knees. The no. 8s can also bind through the splayed legs of the locks and grasp the fronts of their jerseys. This gives a good pushing position as it automatically brings the no. 8s' shoulders into the correct position on the props buttocks.

Progression: When the players are ready to progress, the scrum-half gives a signal for the concerted push. On the words 'ball in' the players bend their knees. On the word 'now' they lower their hips and straighten their spine, and straighten their legs to push. Do not allow any push to go further than 1.5 m, or turn more than 45 degrees.

setting a scrummage in a controlled game environment

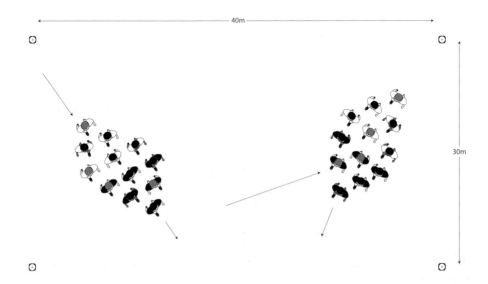

Objective: To develop skills, strength and experience to compete in a full scrum-mage, and to provide a clearly understood and ingrained routine.

Equipment: Four cones and one ball for every 12 players.

Description: Use the cones to mark a playing area approximately 30 m x 40 m. This drill uses the skills already learned, but in a less structured environment, so that the packs have to learn to operate as a unit. The coach calls for a scrum and makes a mark. The two front rows bind together and then stand on it, an arm's length apart. The second rows bind into a pushing position. The no. 8s then kneel on one knee behind them and bind into place. On the 'crouch' command, the forwards take a pushing position and wait for the 'engage' command. They do not push. Repeat the exercise, resetting the packs in different areas of the playing area.

Progression: When you are satisfied that the skill level is high enough, scrum halves can be added using a ball for uncontested scrums. The next stage is to allow the hookers to compete for the ball with scrums pushing. Encourage the no. 8s to control the ball at their feet. Do not allow any push to go further than 1.5 m or turn more than 45 degrees.

TACKLING AND DEFENCE

British and Irish Lions winger Shane Williams tries to evade the tackle of Manawatu defender Jason Campbell during the Lions' 2005 tour of New Zealand.

drill 70 *side-on tackles*

Objective: To introduce the skills required for an effective side-on tackle.

Equipment: Two cones and one ball for every eight players; targets on both thighs of every player.

Description: Divide the players into two teams of four. Each team must line up behind a cone, with the groups at right angles to each other as shown. On the coach's command, player 1 walks out briskly with the ball. Player 2 (the tackler) approaches and executes a side-on tackle. The two players then regain their feet, and run to the end of the opposite line. Players 3 and 4 repeat the drill. When all players have participated, swap sides so that the tackle is executed with the opposite shoulder.

Coaching points: In the approach, instruct the tacklers to keep their head and hands up, and aim for the target sticker. At the point of contact they should hit and wrap hard with the arms. The attacking player is relatively passive during this introductory phase. Do not allow fends or stepping.

Progression: As skills develop, ask attackers to gradually increase their speed to a jog, half pace etc.

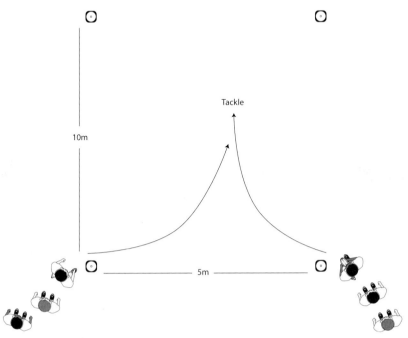

Objective: To introduce the skills required for an effective chase-down tackle.

Equipment: Four cones and one ball for every eight players; targets on both thighs of every player.

Description: Divide the players into two teams of four, and place the cones forming a grid 5 m wide by 10 m long, as shown in the diagram. Each team must line up behind a cone in two parallel lines, and stand approx. 1 m apart. On the coach's command, player 1 walks out briskly with the ball. On the second command, player 2 (the tackler) approaches and executes a tackle from the rear. The two players then regain their feet, and run to the end of the opposite line. Players 3 and 4 repeat the drill. When all players have participated, swap sides so that the tackle is executed with the opposite shoulder.

Coaching points: In the approach, instruct the tacklers to keep their head and hands up, and aim for the target sticker. At the point of contact they should hit and wrap hard with the arms making firm contact and allowing the legs to drag. The tackle should be slightly from the side rather than directly behind. The attacking player is relatively passive during this introductory phase.

Progression: As skills develop, ask attackers to gradually increase their speed to a jog, half pace etc.

drill 72 *head-on tackles*

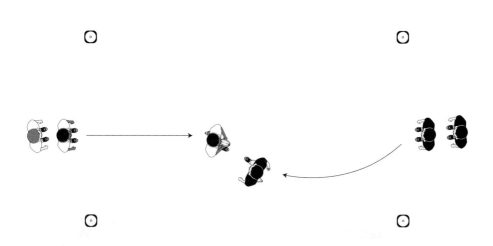

Objective: To introduce the skills required for an effective head-on tackle.

Equipment: Four cones and one ball for every eight players; targets on both thighs of every player.

Description: Divide the players into two teams of four, and place the cones forming a grid 5 m wide by 10 m long, as shown in the diagram. Each team line up between the cones at either end of the grid. On the coach's command, player 1 walks briskly down the centre of the grid with the ball. Player 2 (the tackler) approaches in an arc to force player 1 towards the side of the grid, and then executes a tackle. The two players then regain their feet, and run to the opposite end of the grid to join the back of the line. Players 3 and 4 repeat the drill.

Coaching points: It is important that the tackler approaches in an arc to limit the opportunity for the attacker to evade. Instruct the tacklers to keep their head and hands up, and aim for the target sticker, allowing the legs to drag. The head must go past the thigh or hip, then at the point of contact they should hit and wrap hard with the arms, allowing the legs to drag. The attacking player is relatively passive during this introductory phase. Do not allow fends or stepping.

Progression: As skills develop, ask attackers to gradually increase their speed to a jog, half pace etc.

drill 73 defensive alignment 1

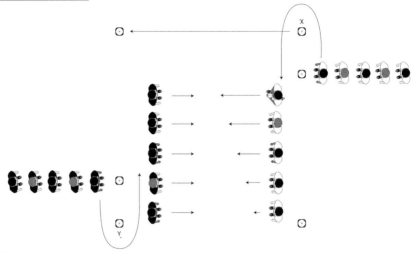

Objective: To create a well structured defensive line from broken play; to develop defensive communication.

Equipment: Six cones and one ball for every eight players.

Description: Divide the players into two teams of four. Set out a 10 m by 10 m grid using four cones, and place two cones 2 m apart on the left boundary. Both teams line up behind their cones (forming the attack and defence) with the ball on cone X. On the coach's command, both attackers and defenders run from the start point around cone X and Y respectively to form an attacking and defensive line. As the attackers round their cone they pick up the ball. Start the drill at a brisk walking pace with the emphasis on communication. The drill is completed when the attack either completes or is broken down.

Coaching points: Defence – there will be a temptation for the first defensive player to run blindly to the far side of the grid, leaving a gap on the inside. Defenders joining the line must make the outside man aware of their presence, allowing him to push out. By joining in the line from the inside, the attacking run made close to the point of breakdown is always defended.

Attack – as attackers will be joining from the side again there is a temptation to take the ball and set off at a 45-degree angle. This will allow the defenders to drift out and will eventually run the attack out of space. Encourage attackers arriving at the breakdown to straighten the line of running to 'fix' the defenders. The timing of runs is important – too early and the only way to go is sideways, which allows defenders to drift out.

Progression: As competence grows increase the pace.

drill 74 *defensive alignment 2*

Objective: To create a well-structured defensive line from broken play; to practise attacking from a breakdown and develop communication.

Equipment: Four cones, two tyres and one ball for every eight players.

Description: Divide the players into two teams of four. Set out a 15 m by 15 m grid using the cones, with two tyres 2 m apart in the centre of one side as shown in the diagram – the tyres represent a breakdown and the two extremes of a ruck, and therefore the offside line for the defenders. Both teams group behind their tyre, and the ball is placed in the attackers' tyre. On the coach's command, both attackers and defenders run from the start point to form an attacking and defensive line. Start the drill at a brisk walking pace with the emphasis on communication. The drill is completed when the attack either completes or is broken down.

Coaching points: Follow the same defence and attack points outlined in drill 73.

Progression: As competence grows increase the pace and increase numbers of players to five per side.

defensive alignment 3

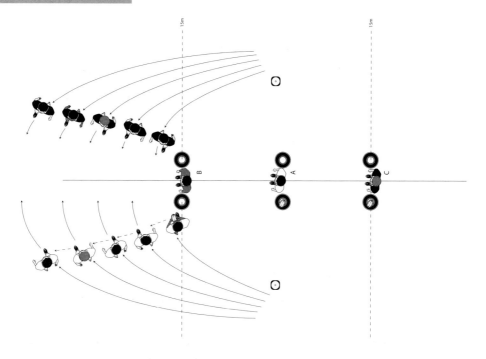

Objective: To create a well-structured defensive line from broken play; to practise attacking from a breakdown.

Equipment: Two cones, six tyres and three balls for every 10–14 players.

Description: Divide the players into two teams of between five and seven. On the 22 m line set two tyres 2 m apart in the centre (A) and two on either 15 m line (B and C). Place two cones 10 m out from the centre tyres (the tyres represent a breakdown and the two extremes of a ruck, and therefore the offside line for the defenders). The two teams (defenders and attackers) group behind the cones, and put a ball in each pair of tyres as per the diagram. On the coach's command ('A', 'B' or 'C'), the attackers run to the designated tyre and start an attacking move from that point. The defenders run to form a defensive line at the same tyre while remaining onside. The attackers can choose the right or left side of their breakdown as the point to attack. The drill is completed when the attack either completes or is broken down.

Coaching points: Ensure that the distances between the 'breakdowns' is in keeping with the age of the players – it's a short, sharp drill, not a stamina run!

drill 76 *defensive line 1*

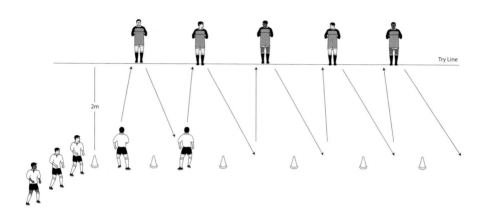

Objective: To introduce defensive alignment.

Equipment: Five tackle shields (each with a target sticker) and six cones for every 12 players.

Description: Divide the players into five attackers and seven defenders. Stand the attackers along the try line at 3 m intervals, each with a tackle shield. Set a line of cones 2 m opposite to create five channels. Defenders line up behind the start cone. On the coach's command, defender 1 jogs from the start cone to tackle attacker 1 – he then quickly recovers and moves back and right to 'mark' attacker 2. Defender 2 then steps in opposite attacker 1, and on the coach's command both players move up together and perform a tackle on their respective attackers. The drill continues until there are five defenders moving up in a line. At this point defender 1 is at the end of the line, and so moves off the grid and returns to the start. In this way the drill can run continuously.

Coaching points: The objective is for the line to move up together. Initially the coach calls the start of the movement, but as understanding grows the player on the left of the drill can call (as this is the point closest to where the ball would be coming from). Ensure that although defenders have to be aware of one another, they have to also concentrate on the tackle skills introduced in previous drills. Tacklers: remember – hands up, heads up, hit the target and wrap with strong arms. Keep rotating attackers and defenders.

Progression: Greater speed can be introduced, but never at the expense of a cohesive line.

Objective: To practise defensive alignment as a group.

Equipment: Five tackle shields (each with a target sticker) and two cones for every 10 players.

Description: Divide the players into five attackers and five defenders. Stand the attackers along the try line at 2 m intervals, each with a tackle shield. Defenders line up opposite the attackers on the 5 m line. The coach stands behind the line of defenders facing the attacking line. When the coach puts a hand out to the right or left, the attacking line shuffles sideways on their line in the direction indicated and the defenders must follow them. When the coach puts both hands in the air, the attacking line jogs forwards as if in attack, the defenders advance together in a line and hit their shield as if to make a tackle. Both lines then retire to the starting position and the drill continues. Only when the attackers advance does the defensive line move up.

Coaching points: The idea is to move the defensive line around to challenge communication and therefore coordination. The defensive line must move together to mark their opposite number. There is a lot going on for the defenders but keep emphasising the tackle cues – head up, hands up, spot the target, hit and wrap.

Progression: Greater speed can be introduced, but never at the expense of a cohesive line.

drill 78 *defensive line 3*

Objective: To improve defensive alignment as a group.

Equipment: Six tackle shields (each with a target sticker) and two cones for every 11 players.

Description: Divide the players into six attackers and five defenders. Stand the attackers along the try line at 2 m intervals, each with a tackle shield. Defenders line up opposite the attackers on the 5 m line (the extra attacker will be the overlap). As in drill 77, the coach stands behind the line of defenders facing the attacking line and signals left, right or advance. The challenge for the defenders is to cope with the overlap attacker by drifting on to the outside player. This is done by initially lining up attacker 1–defender 1; attacker 2–defender 2 etc. with defender 6 as the overlap. As the coach calls the attack to the right, the defenders must shift to mark one player in the line (defender 1–attacker 2; defender 2–attacker 3 etc.). As before, the coach moves the attack both left and right, until he calls the advance and the tackles are made. Then both teams retire and the drill is repeated.

Coaching points: The idea is to move the defensive line around to challenge communication and co-ordination. The defensive line must move together to ensure that no excessive gaps are left in the line. Encourage lots of talking – in a game situation the players on the inside must constantly communicate with the defenders outside them. This allows the defence to drift without having to keep checking that the inside defenders are in place. There is a lot going on for the defenders but keep emphasising the tackle cues – head up, hands up, spot the target, hit and wrap.

Progression: Greater speed can be introduced, but never at the expense of a cohesive line.

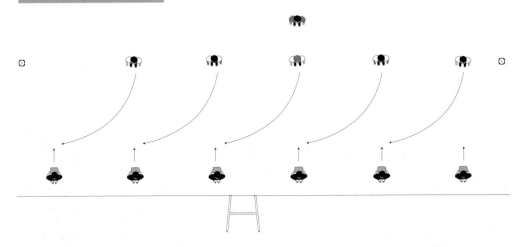

drill 79 advancing defensive line – drift

Objective: To develop defensive alignment as a group in a close-to-live situation.

Equipment: Six tackle shields (each with a target sticker) and two cones for every 11 players.

Description: Divide the players into six attackers and five defenders. Stand the attackers along the try line at 2 m intervals, each with a tackle shield. Defenders line up opposite the attackers at a distance of 10 m, and there is an overlap attacker as in drill 78. As before, the coach stands behind the line of defenders and signals left, right and advance. As before, the coach moves the attack both left and right until he calls the advance and the tackles are made. As the defensive team is further away, when the attack comes in the defensive team comes straight up together on the coach's command and drifts out together to cope with the overlapping attacker.

Coaching points: The defence are not able to drift out as this will create gaps on the inside. This drill imitates the situation where the first player is in possession and is marked until he passes, and then the defensive line moves up and out. Encourage lots of talking – in a game situation the players on the inside must constantly communicate with the defenders outside them. This allows the defence to drift without having to keep checking that the inside defenders are in place. There is a lot going on for the defenders but keep emphasising the tackle cues – head up, hands up, spot the target, hit and wrap.

Progression: Replace the coach's command with a call from the inside defender who can now choose when the 'pass' has been made, and calls the drift.

KICKING AND FIELDING

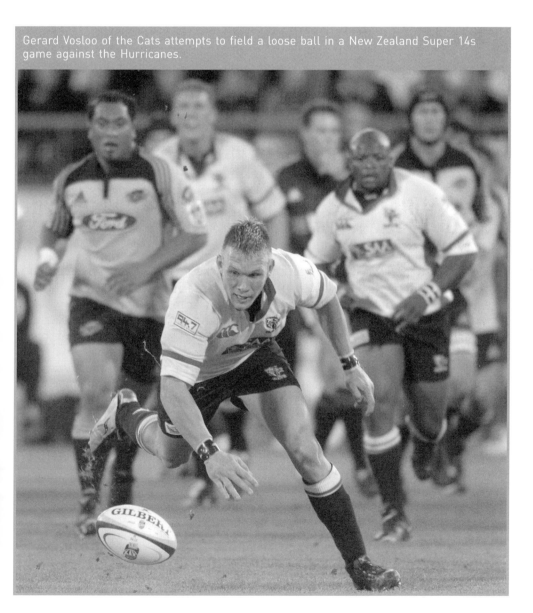

Gerard Vosloo of the Cats attempts to field a loose ball in a New Zealand Super 14s game against the Hurricanes.

drill 80 baseball

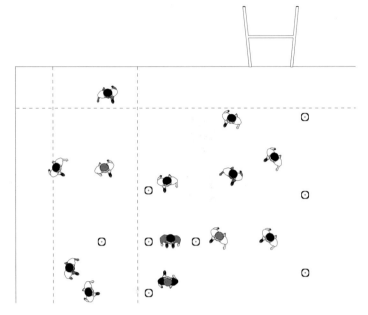

Objective: To challenge the kicker's awareness of space.

Equipment: Five cones and one ball for 12 or more players.

Description: You need at least 12 players for this drill – three are kickers and the rest are fielders with the coach as the bowler. Create a baseball/rounders diamond placing the cone bases 10 m apart with a fifth cone for the 'bowler'. The outfield should be restricted and is best created by using a corner of the pitch, with touchline and tryline as two sides and cones marking out the other boundaries. The coach throws or rolls the ball to kicker 1 who gathers the ball and then immediately kicks into the outfield. Kicker 1 is allowed to keep running as long as the ball has not been fielded. The player is out if caught on the full or 'stumped' on a base (as in rounders) or if the ball goes over the touchline on the full or the dead-ball line.

Coaching points: Once the players have the concept, the coach can use the feed to kicker 1 to test the skill of dispatching the kick quickly. Fielders must communicate to call for the ball clearly and early. Encourage the kicker to aim their kick into a specific space. You may have to adapt the area in which you work to suit the ability of the players.

Progression: Encourage fielders (defenders) to work off the ball. Add a rule that the kicker can only be stopped by the ball being passed through three pairs of hands. This replicates the environment of a back-three supporting a catcher and preparing to counterattack.

attacking kicks skills practice

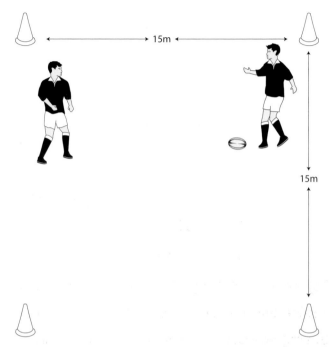

Objective: To explore and practise various types of attacking kick.

Equipment: Four cones and one ball between two or three players.

Description: Place the cones to make a 15 m by 15 m grid. Players execute grubber and chip kicks to one another. Start with only one type of kick, then change over to another. Finally, allow the players to vary their kicks by choice. Do not persist with one type of kick, for too long before introducing variation as the skill set will be driven deeper as the players constantly have to re-visit and re-apply the skills.

Coaching points: As this is an introductory drill it can easily become boring and standards will drop accordingly. Therefore, ensure that groups are very small and that the skills checklist has been clearly stated before the drill starts.

Progression: An element of competition can be introduced by using a scoring system. If the receiver does not have to move his feet to catch, then three points are awarded – if they have to move one foot then only one point is awarded.

attacking kicks – on the move 1

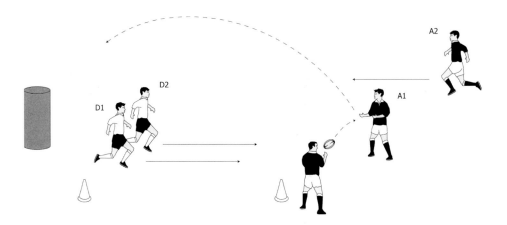

Objective: To develop kicking skills on the run.

Equipment: Two defenders, two attackers, a scrum-half, balls and a tackle bag or shield.

Description: Place the cones 3 m apart to signify the back feet of a ruck or maul. Defender D1 and D2 establish a defensive line with the tackle bag 5 m behind them as the target for the kicking player. Attacker A1 is passed the ball from the scrum-half feeder as from a ruck or maul. Attacker A1 runs onto the ball and kicks through to hit the target bag. The kick can be varied from a grubber kick or a chip. Attacker A2 runs in support to allow defenders to have opposite numbers to mark.

Coaching points: Accuracy is the objective, so build the pace gradually. The aim is to hit the bag. If attacker A1 does not move onto the ball he will not encourage the attackers to advance – the run must provide interest for the defenders. Encourage the defenders to defend as if the kick is not necessarily expected – this drill is for the attackers! Attacker A2 should adjust the angle and timing of his run to put pressure on the catcher (in this case the target bag) without straying offside. Rotate the players after three turns each.

Progression: Initially the defenders advance slowly providing only shape to the drill. As skills improve have the defenders move at near match pace aiming to pressurise the kick. As a final variation, attacker A1 can have the option to pass to attacker A2 if the defenders are leaving him unmarked and focusing too much on the kicker.

attacking kicks – on the move 2

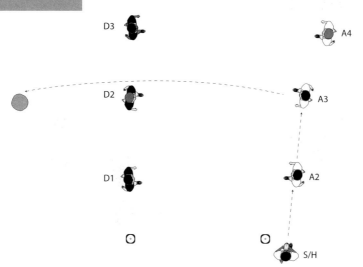

Objective: To develop kicking skills on the run in a game situation; to provide an environment for attacking chasers to time runs.

Equipment: Four defenders, four attackers, a scrum-half (feeder) and balls.

Description: Place the cones 3 m apart to signify the back feet of a ruck or maul. Defenders 1, 2, 3 and 4 establish a defensive line. Attacker A2 is passed the ball from the scrum-half feeder as from a ruck or maul. Attacker A3 receives the ball and kicks through to hit the target bag. The kick can be varied from a grubber kick or a chip. Attackers A2 and A4 run to chase and gather the kick.

Coaching points: Accuracy is the objective, so build the pace gradually. The timing of the outside runners is vital to the effectiveness of this skill – attacker A1 must move onto the ball or he will not encourage the attackers to advance. When he receives the ball attacker A1 must be facing the inside shoulder of defender A1. Attacker A3 should start in a conventional attacking line and advance to take a flat pass. Attackers A2 and A4 must time their run to ensure that they remain onside but break the line at enough pace to be in a position to pressurise the receiver (who in this drill is absent). Rotate one player after two turns until everyone has had a go.

Progression: Initially the defenders advance slowly providing only shape to the drill. As skills improve have the defenders move at near match pace aiming to pressurise the kick. As a final variation attacker 3 can have the option to pass to attacker A2 or A4 if the defenders are leaving him unmarked and focusing too much on the kicker.

Objective: To introduce the skills required to smother and gather a rolling ball.

Equipment: One ball per pair.

Description: Divide the players into pairs. Player 1 stands with their legs shoulder-width apart, and player 2 stands 1 m in front of player 1 with the ball. Player 2 rolls the ball through the legs of player 1 – no more than 5 m. Player 2 runs through and falls on the ball to gather it, recovers quickly and then returns the ball to player 1 at which point the roles are reversed and the drill continues.

Coaching points: Player 2 should aim to fall slightly in front of the ball and slide onto it. The objective is to make the whole body into a 'net' to smother the ball as it bounces rather than to try and simply drop straight down onto the ball. Start slowly so that the process is clearly understood before speeding up the drill.

Progression: Make sure that player 2 practises falling on to both left and right sides by making the initial run past alternating shoulders of player 1. As competence grows the players can experiment by rolling the ball out at different angles and increasing the approach speed. They will soon discover that the harder they fall on the ball the easier it is to use their momentum to regain their feet.

Objective: To develop defensive skills required to smother and gather a rolling ball; to challenge decision-making and communication in a defensive environment.

Equipment: One ball for every three players.

Description: Player 1 stands with legs shoulder-width apart with the ball. Players 2 and 3 stand 1 m in front of player 1. Player 1 calls out a number (to identify player 2 or 3) and immediately rolls the ball backwards through his own legs – no more than 10 m. Players 2 and 3 run through and the designated player falls on the ball to gather it, recovers quickly and then drives into player 1, allowing the supporting player to form a mini-maul to protect the ball. When the ball is well secured the coach halts the drill and the players rotate.

Coaching points: Start slowly so that the process is clearly understood before speeding up the drill. As the drill seeks to replicate a defensive situation the supporting player must work hard to get around the player gathering the ball so that he is in an onside position.

Progression: Once the roles are clear to all players, remove the initial call from player 1 and ask the runners to decide who is best positioned to fall on the ball based on where it rolls and make a loud, clear and early call.

drill 86 scrum-half box kick 1

Objective: To introduce the mechanics of the scrum-half attacking 'box kick' (height and accuracy are key as this kick will be used in games to allow team mates the opportunity to re-gather the ball).

Equipment: Six target cones, one cone and one ball per player (more if possible).

Description: The target cones are placed in a circle as a target grid to land the ball. This grid will vary in size depending on age and competence – start with a big grid (10 m diameter). The kickers set up one cone each around 15 m away from the target circle. The kickers then practise a lobbed box kick into the centre circle. Completed kicks are re-gathered by the players and the drill continues.

Coaching points: Place the ball just behind the cone, and ask the right footed kicker to take up a wide stance with left foot close to the ball. Reach out for the ball and in one movement the left foot steps away to in font of the right and the kick is executed. By swiftly moving the left foot from the ball to in front of the right, room is created for the kick and the need for a backswing is removed, all of which gains time for successful execution.

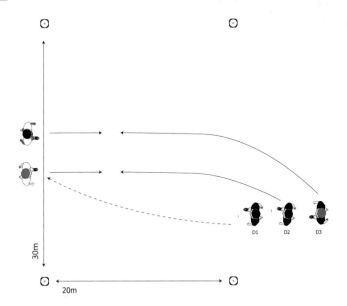

Objective: To develop communication and coordination in players chasing attacking kicks.

Equipment: Four cones, lots of players and balls in a 30m x 20m grid.

Description: Defenders 1–3 stand at one end of the grid, one behind each other. Attackers 1 and 2 set up to receive a kick at the other end of the grid. Defender 1 kicks deep to attacker 1 or 2 who catches, and then they set off up the grid as if counter-attacking. It is the job of attackers 2 and 3 to defend. Players rotate roles frequently to avoid fatigue.

Coaching points: It is vital that the chasing players work together. If one runs up too quickly he will leave a gap that the attackers can exploit. One player running up on their own is easily beaten by a stationary player. Encourage the defenders to be aware of where their partner is while the ball is in the air. Indeed, after an initial 'spot' a runner can gauge where a ball will land and can therefore afford a look around to see where supporting runners and defenders are. If the kick is high and the catcher is isolated (and therefore unlikely to pass), both defending players should stay close together. If the kick is caught early and other counter-attackers are in support, the chasers must communicate to mark both ball carrier and supporting chasers. Chaser/runners *must* be behind the ball when it is kicked.

Progression: Start with two groups of defenders, each with a number 1–4. A designated player kicks the ball and the coach calls random numbers '1s' or '3s' etc. so that the players have to react and form up quickly to chase and defend.

drill 88 scrum-half box kick 2

Objective: To develop the mechanics of the scrum-half attacking 'box kick'; to coordinate the run of the chasing winger.

Equipment: Five cones and as many balls as possible for every pair.

Description: In each pair one player is the scrum-half, and one player is the winger. Set up one cone to represent the rear foot of a scrum/maul. The remaining four cones act as a target grid to land the ball. To gauge how far away the grid has to be, time how long the ball stays in the air from the scrum-half's kick and then measure how far the winger can run in that time. This kick can be used as a defensive clearance but it will be useful to provide context by setting the drill up in an attacking field position, for example at the intersection of the 15 m and 10 m lines. Taking the cue from the scrum-half's approach to the ball, the winger times his run so that he is running at full tilt and just onside when the ball is kicked. Keep rotating wingers so that quality stays high, and practise on both the left and right sides of the pitch.

Coaching points: The aim is for the winger to arrive at the same time as the ball, but this will take some adjustment by the runner to time their run perfectly. Ask resting players to silently critique the working players, which will increase awareness of the skills and help the development of self-coaching. Vary the points on the pitch where this is executed so that the players can see what works and what does not.

Progression: Introduce a defensive and attacking back row to pressurise the kicker. Only do this once the drill is well understood.

CONTROLLED
GAMES

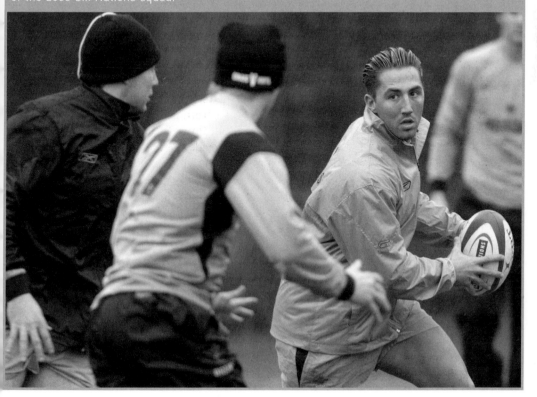

Wales's Gavin Henson looks for an option in a mini-game during training with other members of the 2006 Six Nations squad.

drill 89 *eight-a-side*

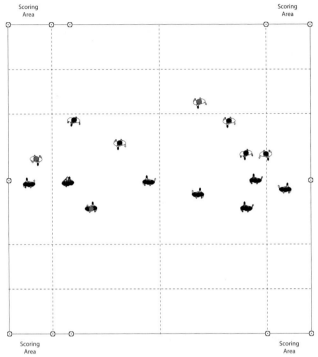

Scoring Area · Scoring Area · Scoring Area · Scoring Area

Objective: To provide opportunities for players to practise specific skills in a contested game environment.

This game is to practise tackling, running and passing and moving the ball away into space creating room for runners.

Equipment: Eight cones and one ball.

Description: On a pitch (no more than half a full pitch), use the cones to mark out the corners and halfway line. Divide the players into two teams of 8–10. The game is played under the full rules of rugby but all infringements plus the ball off the pitch are dealt with by a 'tap' penalty. Kicking is not allowed. The opposition retires 7 m for all restarts. Additional rules are as follows:

- each try is worth 3 points.
- a penalty is awarded for running backwards or across the pitch and running the ball back into congested spaces.
- the strongest runners are not allowed to dominate play. After scoring once they can be awarded a point for every break they make and pass that leads to a try.

Progression: At the corners add a second cone 3 m in from the corner cone. This becomes the only scoring area on the goal line. Strong emphasis is placed on moving the ball wide and not running wide.

drill 90 receiving the kick off – unopposed drill

Objective: To provide opportunities for players to practise restart skills in a game situation.

Equipment: A full XV of players, plus two extra players, two tackle shields, a full pitch and one ball.

Description: The drill begins at the halfway line. Players are set out as shown in the illustration. The coach kicks off with a drop kick to the forwards. A player gathers the ball, makes ground and passes to a team member. Further ground is made into tackle shield (A) and the player goes to ground. A ruck is formed and the ball is played back to the scrum-half. Two passes are made to the inside centre. The centre makes ground into tackle shield (B) and goes to ground. A second ruck and the ball goes through all hands out to the wing. Drill stopped and repeated two or three times. Change the tackle shield carriers.

Coaching points: Facing the kick off, players must ensure that all spaces are covered. The front row to stand on the 10 m line about 5 m apart. The remainder of the forwards take up scrum positions at distances of 5 m from each other. It is easier to be further back from the kick off and have to run forwards, rather than be too close and have the ball go over their heads. For the purposes of this early drill, if the ball does not cross the 10 m line it is not in play.

Progression: Instead of a ruck at the shields, players stay on their feet to form a maul.

drill 91 *making the kick off – unopposed drill*

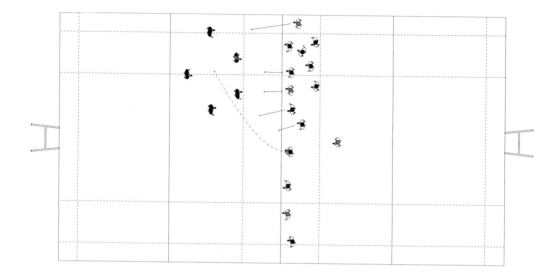

Objective: To provide opportunities for players to practise restart skills in a game situation.

Equipment: A full XV of players, plus 3–6 extra players and one ball.

Description: Use a full pitch for this drill, and play begins at the halfway line. Players are set out as shown in the illustration. A designated player kicks off with a drop kick. The three opposition players attempt to field the ball. The attacking side follows up the kick, and tag tackles the opposition.

Coaching points: The attacking forwards must stay behind the kicker at all times, otherwise they are offside. The kicker must make the ball cross the 10 m line. An ideal kick is high enough to give time for the chasing forwards to arrive as the ball comes down. It is important for the kicker to have good skills with the drop kick. Forwards to start behind the kicker to generate speed. Encourage the backs to come up in a line abreast alongside the advancing forwards to block any movement across the pitch from defenders. Repeat the exercise, changing players and kickers.

Progression: The two drills of 'making a kick off' and 'receiving a kick off' can be combined into an opposed drill. Divide the forwards up into two equal groups. The defending side receives the kick off in the face of the advancing attackers and forms either a ruck or maul. The drill can end at this point. The basic objective of the drill is for people to know what to do at the kick off.

making and receiving the kick off at the 22 m line - unopposed

22m

Objective: To provide opportunities for players to practise restart skills from the 22m line in a game situation.

Equipment: A full XV of players plus 3 extra players, a full pitch and one ball.

Description: Play begins at the 22 m line. Players are set out as shown in the illustration. A designated player kicks off with a drop kick. The three opposition players attempt to field the ball. The attacking side follows up the kick and tag tackles the opposition.

Coaching points: The ball simply has to cross the 22 m line to be in play. Players must stay behind the kicker. The height of the kick is again important to provide time for the chasers. Repeat several times with changes of kickers.

Progression: Divide the players into two groups to practise opposed 22 m restarts.

Objective: To develop drills and skills to operate defensive kicking ability from behind the 5 m line, in the goal area or any defensive position within the 22 m area.

Equipment: One ball.

Description: Divide the players into two sets of forwards, a scrum-half, a kicker and a ball plus 2–3 defending players. Set an uncontested scrum 5 m from any line that replicates the try line and close to the touchline. The defending side puts in the ball, which is heeled, unopposed. The ball is then delivered to a player standing some 5–8 metres directly behind the scrum. He kicks to touch. Players from the opposition scrum attempt to tackle the kicker or charge down the kick. Alternate the forwards to be defending and experiment with kickers.

Coaching points: Communication between the scrum-half and the kicker is vital to ensure each is aware of the other's position. The scrum-half's pass must be flat and accurate to give the kicker time. The kicker should stand at the extremity of the scrum-half's pass to maximise time available for the kick. If the kicker drops the ball he must touch it down immediately. The defending scrum-half should encourage his scrum/maul to put on a push to drive back the opposition. This will keep loose forwards tied down to restrict the push rather than ready to charge the kick.

Progression: Set an uncontested lineout on the 5 m line. The ball is caught, protected with a maul, and then smuggled back to the scrum-half, passed to the kicker, who finds touch.

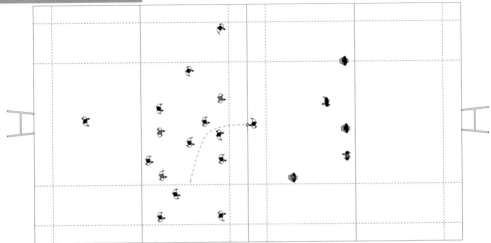

Objective: To accustom young players to the constantly changing structure of the game.

Equipment: A full XV of players plus 4–5 extra players, 2–3 tackle shields and one ball.

Description: Use a full pitch for this drill. Begin with the XV receiving kick off. Spare players offer some token opposition, particularly at lineouts and kick offs. They can carry the tackle shields as and when needed. Players should play as if they have opponents, but the coach uses commands to structure the proceedings:

- **'set'** – the ball carrier turns, as if tackled, and remains on his feet. Forwards maul and smuggle the ball to the scrum-half then out to a backs passing movement.
- **'tackle'** – the ball carrier goes to ground. Forwards ruck ball to scrum-half, to backs or to late arriving forwards.
- **'blind'** – for the scrum-half to go blind.
- **'link'** – ball carrier to link with nearest player.
- **'wide'** – ball to be passed to wings.

With imagination a whole game can be created. The coach can award penalties, defensive and attacking lineouts and scrums, 22 restarts and halfway restarts.

Coaching points: The emphasis must be on support play. Players are not allowed to run too far. Late arriving players at a ruck to decide whether they are needed. If the ball is already won they can hang back to support the three quarters. Discourage forwards 'loitering' between 9 and 10. The correct position is either in front or behind this line so that the scrum-half can choose to release the ball to the backs.

drill 95 *mauling 1*

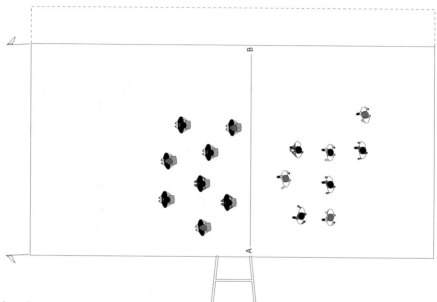

Objective: To accustom players to close-quarter skills required for effective mauling.

Equipment: Eight tackle shields and one ball.

Description: Divide the players into eight attackers, and eight defenders with tackle shields. Set up in a restricted area approximately 10 m x 15 m. The dead ball area is ideal for this drill. The attacking team starts with the ball on line AB, and the defenders with shields stand 2 m in front. On the coach's command, the attacking team run out and set up a maul against the pads. The objective is to get the ball to the other end of the grid to 'score'. The rules are as in a game (offside, collapsing etc.); the only other addition is that the ball cannot be passed, only transferred or smuggled, between players. Defenders must try and force the maul backwards to keep them away from their try-line.

Coaching points: The emphasis must be on correct mauling technique. As there are no defenders competing for the ball there will be little disruption other than the pads forcing the maul back. As in a real game, the coach can stop the drill if the ball becomes locked, or is stopped. If the maul goes to ground the ball must be presented quickly for the next attacker to pick and drive to set up another maul. This can be a very intensive drill and competition is to be encouraged. Remember that you are dealing with young players and allow plenty of rest to ensure that good technique is being practised.

Progression: Dispense with pads and play games with equal sides – full contact.

drill 96 contact skills

Objective: To encourage competitive play in a controlled contact environment.

Equipment: None.

Description: Players lie side by side in pairs, face down on the floor. On the coach's command, players race to get to their feet to try and impede their opponent getting up. They can use any means within the rules of rugby.

Coaching points: This can be developed into a tournament by constantly pairing winners until a 'grand champion' emerges.

Progression: With older/stronger players, start in a press-up position with players facing each other head-to-head. Same rules apply but with option of pulling arms etc.

WARM DOWN

Australia captain George Gregan performs a hamstring stretch during the 2005 Test series against England.

drill 97 *hamstring reach*

Objective: To warm down the body and improve flexibility.

Equipment: One ball per player.

Description: Line the players up along the touchline with feet wider than shoulder-width apart and the ball between their feet. On the coach's command, the players reach down (keeping their legs straight at all times), pick up the ball and place it as far back through their legs as they can. The players then walk backwards until their feet are in line with the ball and repeat the drill. The aim is to cover the given distance (approximately 10 m) in as few pick-ups as possible.

Coaching points: Watch for cheats who bend their legs to gain and advantage! Remind players that this is a slow, controlled race and form is everything.

drill 98 *side stretch*

Objective: To warm down the body and improve flexibility.

Equipment: One ball per player.

Description: Line the players up with their right side facing into a 5 m grid, feet wider than shoulder-width apart, legs straight and the ball in front of their left foot. On the coach's command, the players bend down (keeping their legs straight), pick up the ball and place it in front of their right foot. Then, leaving the ball where it is, the players swap feet, progressing into the grid, so that the ball is by their left foot once more. The movement is then repeated for a set distance – 10 m is more than enough for this drill.

Coaching points: Watch for cheats who bend their legs or pick up with one hand to gain an advantage!

drill 99 *circle stretch 1*

Objective: To warm down the body and improve flexibility.

Equipment: One ball between six players.

Description: Ask the players to form a circle with their feet wider than shoulder-width apart, and their feet touching those of the next players (i.e. right foot to left foot). Keeping their legs straight, all the players reach down and hang their hands as close to the floor as possible. The ball is rolled from one player to another around the circle. After ten passes in total, walk the players around for a minute, then repeat. A soccer ball can be used for easier rolling.

Coaching points: Watch for cheats who are bending their legs to gain an advantage!

Progression: If you have enough players, form two or more groups and race them to see who is first to complete the passes.

drill 100 *circle stretch 2*

Objective: To warm down the body and improve flexibility.

Equipment: One ball between six players.

Description: Ask players to sit back-to-back in a circle with their legs wide apart and feet touching. The ball is passed in order around the circle. Each player must give and take the ball with two hands every time.

Coaching points: This drill provides a stretch to the backs of the legs and requires good flexibility, as each player must rotate their trunk to make the pass. If players lack flexibility, they will creep their bottoms away from the group so that they are leaning back rather than sitting upright. Try and keep the legs nice and straight throughout.

Progression: If you have enough players, form two or more groups and race the first to complete the passes. Vary the direction of passing on command.

drill 101 *giant strides*

Objective: To warm down the body and improve flexibility.

Equipment: Cones.

Description: Players line up facing across a 5 m grid. Mark out a line about 10 m away using the cones. Keeping the body upright, each player takes a slow, controlled stride forwards. The stride should be as long as possible without losing control. Repeat over the set distance and then walk the players back to the start. Repeat.

Coaching points: This drill only works if the body is strictly upright with a 'proud' chest and the head up. In effect, it is an exaggerated running stride. The more slowly this drill is performed, the better. As players over-reach they will twist their body sideways – insist on strict form at all times. The challenge is for each player to beat their own standards – if they can cover the distance in five strides then they should try to cover it in four and a half next time, and so on.